Count Zinzendorf

Count Zinzendorf

A Nobleman With a Heavenly Vision

by Felix Bovet

Translated, Abridged and Adapted by
Rev. T. Alexander Seed
With minor updates by Trudy Harvey Tait

Harvey Christian Publishers, Inc.
449, Hackett Pike, Richmond KY 40475
Tel./Fax (423) 768-2297
E-mail: books@harveycp.com
http://www.harveycp.com

Printed in USA
This Edition 2021

ISBN: 978-1-932774-38-2

Cover Design by
Isaac Samuel
faithgrafikdesigns@gmail.com

Printed by
Lightning Source
La Vergne, TN 37086

Contents

Author's Preface

The name of Count Zinzendorf is inseparable from that of the Moravian Brethren. At the beginning of the eighteenth century—at the time when the Protestants of France were suffering the cruel persecutions for which the revocation of the Edict of Nantes had given the signal—other witnesses to the Gospel were enduring similar suffering in Bohemia and Moravia. The ancient *Unity of the Brethren*, the elder sister of the Churches of the Reformation, seemed at the point of perishing. God did not permit it. Flying from their native land, in order to maintain their fidelity to conscience, the remnants of the Moravian Church found in Zinzendorf a head, an organizer, a defender.

On this ground alone, the life of Zinzendorf would be of great interest. Still, if he had simply been the renovator of the *Unity*, I am not sure that I should have undertaken to write this volume; I should, no doubt, have left it to the members of that church. It is for each family to bury its dead; it is for each people to build the tombs of its prophets.

Besides this historical interest, however, there is in Zinzendorf another interest at once more personal and more general. His character attracts and wins the heart by its elevation and its rectitude; his spirit captivates us by its powerful originality; his simple faith, his zeal, his love for the Lord, the wealth of his experience—these all make his life and his writings an abounding source of instruction and edification. And, what has most of all encouraged me to write this biography, I have learned to love in him a man who, more than any one before him, labored, not from the point of view of any particular church, but for the Church Universal.

Moreover, so far from fading on the horizon of the past, the figure of Zinzendorf is destined, if I do not deceive myself, to stand out more clearly and to be ever better understood. Convinced that it is life which is the light of men, he set himself to bring religion out of the region of abstractions. He endeavored to establish a spiritual union between all Christians, not by inducing them to make concessions and compromises, but by awakening in them a livelier faith and a more ardent love to the Savior. He claimed for all full liberty of conscience. He showed that, without excluding any ecclesiastical institution, faith and love are not limited to any of them and dominate them all—a breadth and largeness of mind the more remarkable in a man who had nothing skeptical about him, and who possessed, in a high degree, the genius for organization. He showed by his example as much as by his ministry that religion is not so much a doctrine as a life, and that the Christian is not a man who merely believes in Christianity but in Jesus Christ.

No doubt the Moravian refugees were the auxiliaries prepared by Providence to second him in his work. But, if it was to them that the New Unity of the Brethren owed its origin, its constitution, and even its principal institutions, it was to Zinzendorf that it owes that universality which has been its glory and which has distinguished it from all other religious communities.

In fact, this Christian liberalism, this need of unbounded brotherhood which were characteristic of Zinzendorf, are to be found in him from the beginning, long before the foundation of Herrnhut. They beam forth in his early relations with the Bishops of France and with the sectaries of Dresden, and long afterwards we see him fighting against a tendency to external aggrandizement which at that time prevailed among the Brethren. He always objected to enlarging the Moravian at the expense of other churches.

Is our age yet liberal enough to appreciate this tendency? It seems, at all events, to be tired of religious divisions, and to perceive that, as Ecclesiastes says, if "there is a time to cast away stones there is also a time to gather stones together" (Eccl. 3:5). It is beginning to feel that there is no need to appeal to theology for a Formula of Concord when Jesus Christ Himself has furnished one: "By this shall all men know that ye are My disciples, if ye have love one to another."

I thought, at first, to limit myself to extracts from the German biographies of Zinzendorf; but, the more I studied his life, the more I became interested in it, and could not content myself with a simple compilation. I went to Herrnhut in order to gather up the traditions of the Count, and to study for myself those institutions which bear so deeply the stamp of his faith and of his genius. I had the happiness to meet there one of the men best acquainted with their history. M.

Louis de Schweinitz, archivist of the Unity, was himself the living archives of the community. He died during my stay at Herrnhut. I ought also to express my lively gratitude to the venerable Bishop Breutel, who welcomed me with so much affection, as well as to all those who so greatly facilitated my researches.

As to the present state of the Church of the Brethren, I have confined myself to a few statistical details in the Appendix.[1] Any judgment on this subject would have been beside my purpose; it is Zinzendorf alone that I have wished to paint.

---

1. This Appendix, consisting of a page of statistical data for the year 1893, has been omitted from this edition.—The Publishers.

Chapter 1

Introductory

Few characters present to the mind so fully as Zinzendorf's that diversity in unity which is said to constitute perfection. Poet, theologian, pastor, missionary, and legislator, influential among the great and living by preference with the little, endowed at once with that warmth of feeling and that vivacity of imagination which lead men to undertake great enterprises, and with that prudence which permits men to accomplish them—he consecrated all his faculties to one end. He had but one thought, one desire, one will—to spread and to revive in men's souls the knowledge of what Jesus Christ has done and suffered for the world. From his early childhood, as he himself relates, he had firmly resolved to devote himself entirely to "that Man Who had given His life for him."

In this aim, this resolution constantly renewed, is to be found the unity of his character and of his life. If, however, there was one among all these talents more striking than another and fitting him more conspicuously for the mission to which God had called him, it was the talent for organization, the art of reading men and leading men—that combination of faculties which makes the statesman. It cannot be doubted that, if he had employed in the service of earthly powers the passionate activity which he consecrated to the service of his divine Master, he would have been one of the most remarkable statesmen of his time.

His enemies often compared him to Cromwell. This comparison, which makes us smile, shows at least that they never denied his political talents. It would have been easy, however, without stepping out of the domain of ecclesiastical history, to find closer and more striking analogies. In the Roman Church, for instance, the character and mission of Ignatius Loyola appear to us to present numerous analogies with the character and mission of Zinzendorf.

Inheriting, like the Biscayan nobleman, the tradition, the taste and the ambition of great things and illustrious enterprises, dowered like him with a poetic and adventurous imagination, with a mystical soul and a passionate heart, he was the knight-errant of the Savior, as Ignatius had been the knight of the Virgin. Each of them founded a powerful society that spread through all the earth, a little church within the Church, an order exercising immense influence in Christendom, an influence more profound than apparent; and both of them made that influence dependent on practically the same means—the education of the young and the work of missions both at home and abroad. It was in these two societies, moreover, that the aggressive spirit of Christianity most quickly and most energetically manifested itself. The Order of Jesuits was no sooner founded than the friends and disciples of Loyola were preaching in India and suffering martyrdom. A very few years after the first Moravian huts appeared upon the slopes of the Houtberg, some of their occupants renouncing their security and their repose, started joyously for the West Indian Islands to proclaim the Savior to the negro slaves.

But if the points of resemblance between these men and these societies be so numerous, where shall we seek for the cause of the no less striking differences which mark the development of the Unity of the Brethren and the Order of Jesus? Why, for instance, have the disciples of Zinzendorf always kept to their humble sphere, far from earthly affairs and ambitions; while the disciples of Ignatius have been found mixing in all the intrigues of courts and cabinets, and, to gain their ends, employing the most questionable means of human policy?

The essential cause of these differences is to be found in the point of departure and in the motto of the founders of these two societies. Ignatius devoted his life to Our Lady; Zinzendorf devoted his life to Jesus. Now, Our Lady is the patron of the Roman Church alone; Jesus Christ is the Head of the Universal Church and the Savior of the world. To labor for the glory of Mary could only be for Ignatius to extend the dominion of the Romish Church, and to drive all heresy away from it. To serve Jesus was not for Zinzendorf to labor for the advantage of any particular church. It was not to bring men within the limits of any external organization, however vast and imposing.

It was to unite all, whatever their differences in doctrine and in ritual, in the bonds of a common love and a common gratitude to Him Who died for our sins and also for the whole world.

Moreover, while the name of the Jesuits is associated with that of the Inquisition, with intolerance and despotism, Zinzendorf is one of the men who have proclaimed most faithfully the principle of Christian tolerance. He was the first, perhaps, to seize clearly the idea of the real unity of the Church amid those diverse denominations—Lutheran, Reformed, Catholic—to which his contemporaries attached so much importance. While Ignatius represents only the principle of authority, and belongs entirely to that Church of the past whose tottering walls his followers attempt to prop, Zinzendorf belongs to the era of liberty and to the Church of the future.

Nor must we forget that Zinzendorf did not found a mere order, but a true society: a society each member of which may acquire property and act on his own account, and in which the family, whilst subordinate to the community, is not sacrificed to it. In this respect, and as the organizer of a community, it is not to the founders of the monastic orders that he must be compared. It is rather to Plato, to Sir Thomas More, and to the modern Socialists, whom he resembles in many points. What they dream about, he realized in part, and here is found another confirmation of the famous saying of Lord Bacon: "What the philosopher is seeking, the Christian has found."

It is the Gospel alone which gives us the solution of the social problem, the reconciliation of order with liberty: for the reconciliation is only to be found in the principle of love, and only the Gospel gives us the audacity to believe in that.

The life of Zinzendorf may be written from many different points of view. Spangenberg, who was his colleague and his successor, wrote it with the twofold end of justifying him from the accusations of his enemies, and of leaving to the community he had founded a memorial of the great benefits which God had conferred on it through him. Most of the biographers of the Count—Reichel, Duvemoy, Verbeek—have written from the special standpoint of their church.... J. G. Müller, the brother of the famous Swiss historian, has given us, in an abridged form but with much intelligence and vivacity, a clear and faithful outline of this remarkable personality. His work is not designed for Moravians only, but for all Evangelical Christians.

All the volumes we have named are written in German. In our turn, we shall endeavor to present to our reader this attractive and original portrait. We shall aim at once to interest them in a powerful individuality and enable them to contemplate in him the sovereign efficacy of the Spirit of God. We shall also aim, in setting forth the relations of Zinzendorf with his contemporaries, to mark out his specific position in the ecclesiastical history of his time.

Chapter 2

Birth, Ancestry, and Religious Environment

Nicholas Louis, Count Zinzendorf and Pottendorf, lord of Freydeck, Schreneck Thürnstein, etc., was born at Dresden on the 26th of May, 1700. His ancestors, raised to the rank of counts of the Empire in 1662, originally belonged to Austria, and are met with in the history of the eleventh century. It was to one of them, Henry de Zinzendorf, that the Margrave of Austria, Leopold the Beautiful, on starting for the Holy Land, entrusted the government of his estates. Another took part in the third crusade, and fought under the walls of Ptolemais. John the Fourth the Younger, Lord of Zinzendorf, embraced Lutheranism on its appearance. In 1633, under the Emperor Ferdinand II, his grandson, Maximilian Erasmus, went into voluntary exile to remain faithful to his faith and to enjoy liberty of conscience. He renounced all his Austrian possessions and retired into Franconia, near Nuremberg. His two sons entered the service of the Elector of Saxony. The elder was a general; the younger, George Louis, became Minister of Council. He was a man beloved and respected by all for his wisdom and for his spotless integrity. He married twice, and from his second marriage sprang Nicholas Louis, whose life we are about to write.

The memory of his ancestors was not without its influence upon the child. The sacrifices made by them for conscience' sake drew down upon his head the benedictions of the Lord. From his infancy, Zinzendorf had habituated himself to estimate the preciousness of that evangelical faith for which his family had sacrificed their worldly goods. It is easy, also, to understand the special sympathy with which he afterwards received the Moravian emigrants. He felt that to him, more than to any other, pertained the duty and the privilege of protecting people who had left their native land and all their dearest earthly interests rather than renounce their faith.

But this was not the only influence of his ancestors. If, in after years, in order that he might not be hindered in the exercise of his ministry, he renounced his title and even his name, he was in his earlier years, quite sensible of the illustriousness of his birth, and of the obligations it imposed.

"I was a Zinzendorf," he says, in one of his poems, "and a Zinzendorf is not worthy to live if he does not spend his life in a good cause. I also bear the name of Christian, and am therefore under double obligation. A Christian ought not to consume himself without giving light." But, in this same poem, how joyfully he sacrifices his family pride at the feet of Him Whom he calls his "only passion."

"Since the time of Count Albert," he says, "the device of our house has been, 'I yield to neither one nor all.' Such is our nature: to yield is painful to us. There is One, however, before Whom my courage is broken: Jesus Who was hung upon the tree, Jesus Who was mocked and outraged, and to Whom the world soon after yielded up its arms."

If it is interesting to know what influence was exerted over Zinzendorf by the social position of his family, it is still more important to study the environment, religious and moral, in which he was placed. In order to do this, it will be necessary to glance at the previous ecclesiastical history of Germany, and at the religious condition of that country at the time of his birth.

So long as the heroes of the sixteenth century had remained upon the scene, the Reformation had conserved some remains of its primitive inspiration, some memory of its glorious origin. After that, the light became obscure, the fine gold dim. Theology took the place of religion and orthodoxy took the place of faith. The history of the German churches is nothing but the history of the laborious formation of the Reformed and Lutheran orthodoxies. One can only get at it through an endless series of quarrels between divers theological opinions. Princes intervened in these scholastic disputes, which produced nothing but subtle formulas and cruel persecutions. The heart sinks when one studies the history of this lamentable epoch, and the sadness it inspires is only tempered by ennui.

This reign of orthodoxy, whose triumph was assured in the Lutheran Church by the Formula of Concord (1577), and in the Reformed Church by the Synod of Dort (1629), continued through the seventeenth century. The seventeenth century is the Middle Ages of the Evangelical Churches of Germany; it is the epoch of Protestant Scholasticism. This tendency did not fail to bear its fruits. The Christian life seemed at the point of disappearing. The Church was dying, dying orthodox. What it needed this time was not a reformation but a revival. And the Revival came. Its center was the same province of Saxony that had been the cradle of the Reformation. Its instrument was Spener.

The work of Spener was essentially practical, the work of a pastor rather than of a theologian. It sought, it is true, to place the study of Scripture in its rightful place, and to temper the despotic authority of the princes and the clergy by creating in the Church a third estate. But he did not dispute the principles of the Augsburg Confession of Faith, the Creed of the Church to which he belonged. His aim was to make his contemporaries feel that the true domain of Christianity is not the intellect, but the conscience, and that faith is not the adhesion of the intellect to a certain number of revealed verities, but an efficacious and regenerating power. Conversion, consequently, was the center of his teaching and the criterion of Christianity. He did not divide men into orthodox and heretic, but into the converted and the unconverted.

Justification by faith preserved in this system the supreme place given to it by Luther, but Spener attached more importance to Christian asceticism than did the great reformer. In him, and in his disciples, both in their preaching, and their life, there was an accent of severity, almost of moroseness—something that reminds us of the Jansenism of Port Royal and the Calvinism of Geneva.

The doctrine of Spener was designated Pietism—a characteristic name enough, inasmuch as the essential point in it is the exclusive importance of piety, that is of individual and practical, as distinguished from general and objective religion. The name was also given to Spener and his associates because of the little meetings for devotion and edification which they were accustomed to hold under the name of *collegia pietatis.*

The austere and powerful speech of Spener, responding to the voice of conscience and confirmed by the Spirit of God, soon echoed throughout Germany. The people were tired of barren disputations. But, while the revival initiated by Spener made its influence felt among the laity, on the people first and then upon the higher ranks of society, the theologians remained, for the most part opposed to the new tendency. The pulpits, both in the churches and at the universities, were closed against its partisans.

The Elector of Brandenburg, Frederick III (afterwards Frederick I of Prussia) became the protector of Pietism. He called Spener, who had incurred the displeasure of the Elector of Saxony, to Berlin, and he founded at Halle, in 1694, a rival university to that of Wittenberg, and one that was destined to represent the new tendency. Halle, henceforward, was to be to the work of Spener what Wittenberg had been to the work of Luther, and it was in this town that Pietism bore the choicest fruits.

But it is with the human mind when God enables it to grasp some truth as it is with children or with savages when some one gives to them a compass or a watch. They are absorbed in it; they put it to all sorts of uses. They never rest till they have spoiled it. The human mind when in possession of some new truth is not content till it has turned it into an error. Every tendency, every school, every church in this way parodies itself. In this way the pietists exaggerated or rather falsified and denaturalized piety itself, just as the orthodox had exaggerated orthodoxy, and as we shall see the disciples of Zinzendorf transform into puerility that Christian simplicity which had been their most precious treasure.

The asceticism of Spener soon became in most of his disciples, a spirit of minute and pharisaic legalism. Starting from the plausible principle that every act is consequential, they came to magnify the importance of the most insignificant actions, to regulate everything, and to make the Christian life consist in the performance of certain acts of devotion, and in the renunciation of certain so-called worldly pleasures. The little devotional meetings, which Spener wished to be "little churches within the Church," came to regard themselves as the only Church, outside which there was no salvation. Hence a most intolerant spiritual pride which compensated the little for their lack of worldly position, and which in the great, nurtured their exclusiveness.

We shall see these aberrations of pietism manifesting themselves in deadly opposition to Zinzendorf and his work. At the moment of his birth, however, the revival was still in its pristine purity. It had exercised its influence on the family of Gersdorf to which his mother belonged. His father, who had been a friend of Spener's at Dresden, was faithful to him in his disgrace. Spener came from Berlin to act as one of the sponsors at the baptism of the young Count.

Chapter 3

Early Years

Zinzendorf was only six weeks old when his father died. His mother was a woman of great merit, of a grave and pious spirit, and of brilliant faculties. She had received a wide and varied education—an education, rare in those days for women. She knew Greek, Latin, and the living languages. She was familiar with the theological sciences, and had a remarkable talent for poetry. This distinguished lady, however, had but little to do with the education of her son. She married again, and went with her second husband, General (afterwards Field-Marshal) Natzmer, to Berlin. Zinzendorf had a profound respect for her, mingled with fear and affection.

"In all my affairs," says he, "my first thought has always been what will best please my mother?" Elsewhere he tells us that he honored her rather as a subject than as a son.

General Zinzendorf, the uncle and tutor of the young Count, did not take a very active part in his early education. The boy was left largely under the direction of his maternal grand-mother, the Baroness Gersdorf. She was, like her daughter, as much distinguished by her talents as by her piety. She was familiar with the leaders of Pietism, and kept up a regular correspondence with them. Spener, Franke, Anton, and Canstein were the friends of the house. The benediction of these servants of God rested, from his earliest years, upon the head of Zinzendorf. Spener, one day, seized with a sort of prophetic inspiration, laid his hands upon him and specially consecrated him beforehand to the kingdom of Jesus.

Not many incidents of his childhood have come down to us, but there is one that so beautifully illustrates his tender-heartedness, his courage and his resourcefulness that we must not pass it by:

> One day, while playing with his hoop near the banks of a deep river which flowed near the castle where he lived, he spied a dove struggling in the water. By some means the poor bird had fallen into the river and was unable to escape. The little Count quickly rolled down a washing-tub which had been left near the water's edge, jumped into it, and, though generally very timid on the water, by the help of a stick he managed to steer himself across the river to the place where the dove lay floating and struggling. With the bird in his hand, he guided the tub back and got safely to land. After warming his little captive in his bosom, the boy ran with it into the wood and set it free.
>
> His mother, who had anxiously watched her boy from a window of the castle, now came out. "Were you not afraid?" she asked. "Yes, I was rather," he answered, "but I could not bear that it should die so. You know, mother, its little ones might have been watching for it to come home."

The child was delicate, but of an energetic will and of an ardent disposition. His natural impetuosity, however, was tempered by a precocious tendency to meditation. He had a lively imagination, and expressed himself with rare facility:

> My genius was simple, but natural. I had a good memory, a spirit rather quick than phlegmatic, a mind calm enough to balance the reasons for and against a matter, a naive intention that would have prospered if reflection had been less scrupulous. An inclination to what was solid and a love for what was true modified my rhyming fantasy.

Notwithstanding his excellent memory, his progress was slow, for his imagination diverted his attention, but the religious sense was developed early. His grandmother and his aunt, as well as his tutor, taught him to pray and instructed him so well in the truths of religion that, when he was only four years old, he knew all the principal points of Christian doctrine. The thought that Jesus is our Brother, and that He had died for us charmed and fired his childish heart. He reasoned quite simply, that since Christ is our Brother we may live with Him in the utmost intimacy. In his *Sermons to Children,* he says:

> I have had the happiness to know the Savior by experience from my earliest years. It was at Hennersdorf, while I was yet a

> child, that I learned to love Him. I heard Him speak continually to my heart. I saw Him with the eyes of faith. They told me that my Maker had become Man, and this touched me profoundly. I said to myself: "If nobody else in the world cares for the Lord, I will give myself to Him. I will live and die with Him."
>
> For many years I have lived with my Savior in this childlike way, talking to Him for hours together as we talk with a friend, walking about in my room absorbed in my meditations. In my conversations with my Savior when a child, I felt happy and grateful to Him for all the good He had wished to do me by becoming Man. But I did not wholly understand the greatness and sufficiency of His meritorious sufferings. The impotence and misery of my nature were not at that time fully revealed to me. I wished myself to contribute to my salvation.
>
> At last, one day, I felt myself so deeply moved by all that my Maker had suffered for me that I shed floods of tears and gave myself up to Him more thoroughly and with more tenderness than ever before. I continued to talk to Him when I was alone. I firmly believed He was near me and I said to myself, "He is God and He will understand me when I cannot express my meaning. He knows my heart." Behold in what immediate personal relations I have lived with God for more than fifty years, and every day I feel the happiness of such a fellowship yet more and more.

This lively faith bore its fruits, and the child sought to bear witness to its reality by all his conduct. Readily acknowledging his faults and compelling himself to correct them, laying himself out to oblige those around him, grateful for the services they rendered him, affectionate, benevolent, with an open heart and hand for all, such was Zinzendorf from childhood.

In childhood, too, this saint and hero was exposed to fierce assaults of doubt. In his cradle, as it were, he had to wrestle with that formidable serpent which tried to strangle him within its coils. He resisted it, and conquered it. He writes:

> I was in my eighth year, when one evening a psalm that my grandma had sung before retiring to rest plunged me into such meditations and then into such profound speculations that I could not sleep all through the night. I saw nothing, heard nothing, so absorbed was I in my thoughts. The most refined ideas of atheism rolled through my soul. They took such a hold upon me, they

> so dominated me that all the infidel doubts that I have met with since have seemed poor and weak in comparison, and have made no impression on me. But my heart remained sincerely attached to the Savior, and I thought again and again that, even if it were possible that there should be another God than He. I would rather be damned with Him than be with the other in Heaven....
>
> The Son of God is my Savior, of that I was as sure as I was of my five fingers. I had loved Him so many years. I had so often invoked Him! So many experiences sweet and bitter, so many prayers answered, so many acts of thanksgiving passed before my mind! What I believed was dear to me; what I thought was odious. I there and then formed the resolution to make use of my reason in things human, and to develop it to the utmost; but in things spiritual, I determined to hold firmly and simply to the truth my heart had seized, to found all other truths on it, and to reject instantly all that I could not deduce therefrom.
>
> It was thus that God created in me the resolution not to spend my life in vain, crude speculations, but to occupy myself with things that tend to edification, to enter into a communion with Him so close and intimate that all my thoughts of Him should be sweet, and to adjourn the consideration of these mysteries until I should be more mature.

Preoccupied with one thought, "burning," from his infancy almost, "to preach the eternal Divinity of Jesus," he saw before him only one career: "In my tenth year I resolved to study theology, and to have no other profession than that of preaching Jesus Christ. But the Lord diverted me from that career until my four-and-thirtieth year. Why? He knows."

In point of fact, his relatives marked out a different path for him. They thought a child so gifted ought to tread in the footsteps of his fathers, and take office in the State. They wished at once to educate him for his high station in life, and to keep him under Christian influences. They therefore selected the *pædagogium* (boarding school) at Halle to which he was sent in 1710.

Chapter 4

School Days

At that time the education of children had nothing of that softness and indulgence which was afterwards introduced into it by the Pelagianism of Rousseau and the sentimentalism of his disciples, the influence of which, for good and evil, has spread through all modern systems. The rude discipline of the sixteenth and seventeenth centuries still prevailed, and nowhere was it applied more harshly, perhaps, than in the *pœdagogium* at Halle. Pietism, whose fundamental doctrine was the entire corruption of human nature, made all education to consist in combating that nature, in mastering it, in humbling it. Zinzendorf would have more than most others to suffer under that pitiless method.

When he arrived at Halle, he was presented to the pious Professor Franke as "a very sharp, intelligent youth, on whom it would be necessary to keep a tight rein, lest he should become too proud and presume too much upon his talents." The directors of the college treated him accordingly. They pretended to prefer to him young men much less advanced than he. For the slightest negligence they inflicted on him the severest punishment. They attributed to him intentions which never entered his mind, and, finally, they sought by all means to render him ridiculous in the eyes of his comrades. Spangenberg writes:

> I do not wish to judge this method. All I know is that it is not by these humiliations which come from man that the heart is made really humble. That is a grace which comes from Jesus Christ. I believe, however, that God permitted the young Count to be treated in this way for his greater good. Still, if he had not already had grace in his heart, this harsh treatment would either have embittered him, or rendered him timid. As it was, it drove him to the Savior, and

> turned him for a time from men, to whom he otherwise might have become too much attached.

The severity of the professors was at least inspired by real love to their pupils. The greatest torment Zinzendorf had to suffer at that period came from his private guardians. Hofmann and Crisenius, who successively filled that office, were, he declares, hypocrites who treated him in the most absurd and barbarous fashion. But the soul of the youth was too firmly grounded to be shaken. "They will not crush me; they will lift me," he exclaims.

The fact is that his heart was so completely occupied by his one great passion that he cared little for external things. The cause of Christ was already the constant object of his thoughts and efforts. He had become connected with a few young men of similar aims. He tells us:

> We had formed little societies. We used to meet to encourage and to help each other to grow in grace and to do our duty. We knew no other way than that laid down in Scripture. It was by this rule that we tested our actions, and, on occasion, we prostrated ourselves before that Invisible Majesty Whom we called our Love, our Brother, and our Head. We asked of Him all that we needed, and we begged of Him especially to make us all that He would have us be.

Seven associations of this kind were formed successively during his stay at Halle, and in all of them he was the last to remain. But he did not stop there. The romantic tendency of his imagination, which also tinged his piety, inspired in him the idea of founding, along with a few friends, a sort of knighthood. The members of the order at first took the name of "Slaves of Virtue," then of "Confessors of Christ"; finally they preferred to call themselves "The Order of the Grain of Mustard Seed."

The members engaged faithfully to confess the doctrine of Jesus in their words and conduct, to love their neighbor, and to take upon their hearts the conversion of others, including Jews and pagans. The insignia of the Order consisted of a medal bearing on one side an *Ecce Homo*—an image of the wounded Christ, and on the other, the inscription: *Nostra medela*—our wounds. This was an obvious refrence to Isa. 53: Christ's wounds—our healing. The Order also had a ring on which was written in Greek: "None of us liveth unto himself." When the members of the Order were afterwards scattered in France, in Switzerland, in Holland, and in Hungary, the Count kept up, by means of correspondence, the sacred bond that bound them in this Gospel chivalry.

A still closer and a life-long friendship united him to a young Swiss, Baron Frederic de Watteville, of Berne. He says:

> In 1715, two young men (Watteville and himself) pledged themselves to labor for the conversion of the heathen, and especially those heathens for whom no one cared. Their idea was not to accomplish this work themselves, for both of them had been destined by their parents to live in the world, and they knew not but to obey. But they hoped that God would point out to them men capable of doing great things.

Though the activity of Zinzendorf at this period bears the imprint of his individuality and might be accounted for by his natural temperament and Christian zeal, one must not underrate the influence of his environment:

> My zeal for the cause of the Savior was powerfully fortified by the opportunity I had daily at Halle of listening to tidings of the kingdom of Christ, of conversing with witnesses to the Gospel from all parts of the world, of making the acquaintance of missionaries, and of seeing persecuted or captive Christians. I also had under my eyes the institutions of Franke, then at their best, and the joyous activity of that man of God. All this deeply imprinted on my heart the desire to suffer for Christ, faith in deliverance, and the disposition to be content with little.

It will be seen that all the characteristics of Zinzendorf—his faith, his zeal for the salvation of the heathen, his organizing genius—are to be found in him during the years of his adolescence. Already, also, his poetical talent had manifested itself. Poetry was his favorite recreation, or rather the most natural expression of his thought. His *verve* was prodigious and the abundance of his inspiration surpassed the swiftness of his pen. This side of Zinzendorf's genius cannot be too often noted. Poetry was a powerful auxiliary in his after work. For every festival of the Church of the Brethren, for each anniversary, in every circumstance which he wished to commemorate, he improvised a psalm or a hymn, and the sentiments of his soul, flying from lip to lip on the wings of poetry, soon became the sentiments of all the members of his Church. The creation of Herrnhut makes us think of the building of the walls of Thebes to the music of the lyre of Amphion.

The progress of Zinzendorf had been rapid. The time had come when it was judged that he was sufficiently prepared for the university. He therefore left the *pœdagogium* in April 1716.

Chapter 5

University Career

On his return from Halle, Zinzendorf spent some weeks with his grandmother at Gross-Hennersdorf. He spent the greater part of the time in the library, reading the works of Luther and other theological treatises. From there he went to Gavernitz to see his uncle, the General. In spite of his ardent desire to give himself up to the study of divinity, he was not permitted to do so. His uncle, who was also his guardian, not only insisted on his studying law instead, but claimed to select the university at which he should graduate.

Halle and Wittenberg at that time represented two rival schools. At Halle, as we have seen, the Pietism of Spener flourished, while Wittenberg, considering itself the privileged guardian of the tradition of the Reformers, maintained in its purity the Lutheran orthodoxy. Zinzendorf having been nourished on the doctrine of Spener, was attracted to Halle; the General preferred to send him to the rival university.

However hard this decision might appear, the young Count submitted to it, and we believe he had his reward, for his sojourn at Wittenberg had the happiest effect on his later development. The comparison he was enabled to make between the two tendencies enlarged his ideas, and raised them to a point of view superior to that of his masters. Had he remained at Halle, he would probably have been a mere successor of Spener. As it was, he rose above both Pietism and Lutheranism, and arrived at a conception of the Gospel, larger, deeper, and more spiritual, than that of almost any other Christian of his time.

On the 7th of September, 1716, Zinzendorf matriculated in his new *Alma mater.* When it became known at Halle that he was studying at Wittenberg, everyone was scandalized. No one knew that he had gone there against his wish, and all cried out upon him for his supposed ingratitude and treachery. He nonetheless remained attached to his former teachers. He felt himself a stranger at Wittenberg. He was always, as he himself declared, "a strict Pietist." He took the part of the Halle divines whenever they were attacked, and suffered much because of his love to them. An assiduous reader and propagator of the writings of Franke, he translated into French his *brochure* on prayer, and himself wrote many religious treatises, one in particular, against the doctrine of "indifferent works." He even pronounced a public eulogy on Spener.

The Wittenbergers tried to turn him from what they called his exaggerated piety, but this only made him more of a Pietist than ever. He felt his faith to be menaced and saw that he ran the risk of losing the treasure which had been his glory and his joy. He was also becoming restless, and began to lose confidence in himself and others. His piety, in this way, lost some of its simplicity, and became, so Spangenberg asserts, more legal than evangelical. He gave himself to ascetic exercises, spent whole nights in prayer and meditation, and set apart a day each week for fasting and solitude.

This first year at Wittenberg was one of the saddest of his life. Obliged to devote himself to studies for which he had no taste; subject to the directions of a tutor whose treatment was enough to "plunge him into despair if it did not drive him to madness"; always on guard against himself, against the world, and against the prevalent theology, Zinzendorf found himself completely isolated and deprived of all community of ideas or of feelings with those around him.

Nothing was more contrary to his loving disposition and to his need of sympathy. Such a state of things could not endure. By and by he came to understand the Wittenbergers better. The prejudices he had conceived against them melted away. He discovered in many of them, in spite of their differences of system, the same living faith, the same Christian spirit as that which animated the Halle professors, and before long, he began to ask himself whether it was not possible to effect a reconciliation between these two inimical factions. The need for Christian unity and fraternity, the desire to bring together into one flock the children of God dispersed in the world or separated by systems and by prejudice, was always uppermost in the mind of Zinzendorf.

We shall soon see him holding out a friendly hand to his brethren in the Roman Church. What then must have been his grief to see Christians of the same communion employing their talents, and expending their energies in persecuting each other, and in destroying each other's influence for good!

It is a beautiful instance of the holy audacity of faith to see this student of seventeen undertaking single-handed to appease hatred so inveterate, and to put an end to a religious war that had been envenomed by thirty years of theological disputations and of pious injuries. Zinzendorf did not hide from himself the difficulty of the task or the slenderness of his resources, but he felt strengthened and encouraged by the benediction on the peacemakers, and set himself to work.

His first attempts were more successful than he had anticipated. His representations were favorably received both at Halle and at Wittenberg, and he formulated a project of accommodation on which both parties might agree. An interview was actually arranged between Drs. Wernsdorf and Franke, and Zinzendorf was to accompany the former to Halle, when his mother interposed and forbade him to proceed with the enterprise. Remonstrance was vain. His mother, acting under unhappy and prejudiced advice, was inflexible, and the plan which her son had formed with so much zeal and charity was abandoned.

In the midst of all this theological and ecclesiastical activity, the young student faithfully conformed to the plan of studies and of conduct formed for him by his tutor. His reluctant mind bent itself to the arid study of Pandects and of Canon Law. He also studied philosophy and physics. He avoided mathematics, for which he had little taste, and applied himself to Hebrew, in which, however, he made but little progress. Greek was familiar enough to him. He spoke Latin with great facility, but French was his favorite language. In this his journal and most of his letters were written. The theses he had to maintain were borrowed by preference from the domain of ethics.

On one occasion, he took as a topic the famous proposition of La Rochefoucauld: "Self-love is the source of all our passions."

The Count was also compelled to learn to fence, to ride, and—to dance! These, as he wittily remarked, were exercises of patience. He applied himself to them, however, for he desired to make rapid progress in them so as quickly to get rid of them and to devote himself to more useful occupations. As to games, he only cared for those that developed the reflective powers, such as chess, or that gave the body salutary exercise, such as tennis or billiards. He did not like to play for money. If, however, his companions insisted on it in order to give additional interest to the game, he consented on condition that they would agree, beforehand, to give their gains to the poor or employ them in the purchase of Bibles for free distribution.

After keeping five terms, Zinzendorf left the University in the spring of 1719. His tutor desired that he should travel in order to complete his law studies in foreign schools, and especially that he might see the world. This was agreed to by the friends of Zinzendorf, but a new tutor was appointed to accompany him.

Chapter 6

Seeing the World

It was not without apprehension that he set out on his travels. He had seen quite enough of the world at Wittenberg to inspire him with a wholesome dread. He feared its temptations, for he felt himself inclined to them, like all the rest of us. Had it depended on his own will, he would have preferred not to take this particular journey. "I wish to die to the world," said he. "What is the good, therefore, of giving myself such pains to live in it?" He submitted, as usual, but he firmly resolved to "hold fast that which he had received." "If it is to make me worldly that they wish to send me into France, it will be money wasted, for God in His mercy will maintain in me the desire to live only for Jesus Christ."

The journey began with Holland. His half-brother proposed to accompany him, and was eagerly accepted as a companion. "During the journey," we read in his journal, "my soul was raised above all earthly things; all my desires were towards Jesus: eternity alone filled my thoughts."

They passed through Frankfort-on-the-Maine, where Spener, who was ever dear to him, had preached, and came to Dusseldorf where they visited the famous picture-gallery. One picture in particular riveted his attention. He says:

> It was an *Ecce Homo* with an admirable expression, above which are found these words:
>
> "I suffered this for thee:
> What hast thou done for Me?"
>
> I felt that I had done very little, and begged my Savior to compel me to suffer with Him if I did not consent to do so voluntarily.

On his nineteenth birthday (May 26th, 1719), he reached Utrecht, and, after visiting a few towns in the vicinity, spent some months at the university. Without neglecting the law course, he ardently pursued some other studies, medicine in particular, which had always many attractions for him. It was also at Utrecht that he learnt English.

Zinzendorf's health had never been robust and in Holland it often failed. His disposition, also, felt the effects of illness, and his thoughts were often turned towards the future life. It was at this time that he adopted *Œternitati* (Eternity) as his motto.

The tidings of the death of Baron of Canstein, who had been Zinzendorf's ideal, made a deep impression on his mind, and supplied new food to his meditations on the eternal repose of the children of God. On hearing of his end, the Count composed a poem in which is embodied his idea of death. He always regarded death as a departure "to be with Christ, which is far better," and his cheerful views have been perpetuated in the teachings of the subsequent Moravian Church. In no other Christian community has death been so completely stripped of its terrors.[2]

The sojourn of Zinzendorf at the University of the Reformed Church contributed in the happiest way to his theological development. As at Wittenberg his Pietistic prejudices against the Lutherans had been dispersed, so at Utrecht he was not slow to recognize the essential harmony at bottom between the parties then so hostile, the Lutheran and the Reformed. At Paris, we shall presently see him taking a further step and pursuing the search after complete Christian unity by entering into the most intimate bonds of brotherly love with the dignitaries of the Roman Church.

In devoting his efforts, at this time and later, to the task of bringing together the members of different Christian communions, Zinzendorf no longer hoped to secure a fusion between them by way of transaction or compromise. He abandoned the idea of such a reconciliation as he had formerly dreamed of between the Pietists

2. It was the fearlessness of the Moravian emigrants in the storm on the Atlantic, it will be remembered, that made such a deep impression on John and Charles Wesley, and led them to see that there was something to be had in the way of religious assurance that they had not obtained.—TR.

and the Orthodox. Many great minds at that period yielded to this chimerical hope, and failed in their attempts.

But in order to hold out a brotherly hand to a member of another church, Zinzendorf had not to wait until they had discussed the various articles of his Creed. He had found in Jesus the unique object of the Gospel. He found in Him also the real and permanent unity of the Church of all times and of all countries. He could henceforth live in perfect communion with Christians of every name, while remaining strictly faithful to the principles which he himself had recognized as true.

In the beginning of September, Zinzendorf left Utrecht and went to Amsterdam and the Hague. Thence he rapidly visited Rotterdam, Antwerp, Malines, Brussels, Valenciennes, and Cambrai, and finally found himself in Paris. He arrived there on September 27th, 1719, and alighted in Rue Saint-Honoré, at the Hotel des Escarelles.

Chapter 7

Paris. Love and Disappointment. Coming of Age

The Count very soon found that he had reached the city at a most interesting juncture. It was about the middle of the Regency. The court and the city, weary of the august monotony of the last years of the great reign, was compensating itself for a long restraint by plunging, at the heels of the Regent, into all the stupidities of a life of pleasure and into the most chimerical novelties. It was the time of Law's Bank speculations, and foreigners from all parts contended with Parisians for the entrance to the Rue Quincampoix and for the Mississippi shares. During the six months Zinzendorf was in Paris he witnessed the culmination and the fall of that strange scheme.

The Church was not less agitated than society. The Bull *Unigenitus*[3] and the affair of the Appellants were at that time occupying every mind, and Zinzendorf also witnessed the last resistance and the final defeat of Gallican liberty.

It will be seen what a vast field of observation Paris furnished to a young man of quick intelligence, whose rank opened to him an entrance at Court, and whose religious and theological development rendered him capable of entering with zest into the ecclesiastical question of the moment. It will also be manifest that a young man of nineteen with a heart full of passion, with an exuberant imagination, with many external advantages, loved and sought by all, would be exposed to manifold temptations. One cannot but admire the strength of his faith, which kept him true to his principles and unspotted from the world. He says:

---

3. A papal bull condemning the doctrines of Jansenism, a dissident religious movement within France.

The more I went into the world, the more closely I clung to the Savior, and the more closely He drew me into the contemplation of His sufferings. Among the great ones of the earth (I knew few of the little at that time), I only sought after those with whom I might celebrate the grace of my Savior. I often found them where I least expected.

With those who did not inspire me with sufficient confidence I kept my distance and was simply polite to them. As for those who wished to lead me into evil, I resisted them without a moment's parley, and disabused them once for all. To this day, I am reaping the fruits of that decision and promptitude. I took no step without expressly consulting my Savior. At Paris, I was in my element. I found myself in relations with ecclesiastics, pious ecclesiastics of all ranks and of no rank, simply clergy or religieux, and with a few ladies "who had grace."...

The world did not know in what category to place me. Some said I still "retained the innocence of my baptism." The evil-thinkers let me pass for a Pietist, but the Pietists did not recognize me as one of them. As for me, it seems to me that if they had presented all the temptations in the world before me, they would not have arrested me for an instant. Ignorance has sometimes been a snare to me, while the knowledge of human misery and of the inventions of the Enemy to fashion us in his likeness has always been the surest preservative.

Zinzendorf felt little disposed, at first, to associate with the higher French clergy. The vices of some of them, the pomp of all, shocked him. But there were a few exceptions. Some of the bishops and at least one cardinal—Cardinal de Noailles—pleased him greatly and were evidently very gracious to him:

When they saw that they had to do with a man to whom religious disputations were repugnant, they evaded them, and plunged with me into the unfathomable ocean of the sufferings and merits of Jesus and of the grace that He has bought for us. In this way, we passed together half a year. The heart was satisfied, and we never dreamt of enquiring to what religion we belonged.... Since that time, I have always set myself to discover the good there is in each religion, for I know that in every nation the Savior has those who love Him.

This habit, I admit, has alienated from me my good friends at Halle, but it has served to advance the Kingdom of Christ. It is

> asked whether the Catholics and the Reformed may be saved while keeping to their religion. Assuredly! But it does not follow that all religions are equally good, still less that one should change his religion when once he has proved it to be a true one, for one that he sees to be erroneous.

Zinzendorf left Paris in the spring of 1720 for Oberbirg, where he spent most of the summer with his aunt, the Countess Dowager of Polheim, passing thence to Castell, the home of another aunt, with whom he proposed to remain for a week. His stay extended over a couple of months. During the fever which was the occasion of this prolonged sojourn, he made the acquaintance of the youngest daughter of his hostess, his cousin Theodora, with whom he fell in love, and to whom he offered his hand. He was not exactly refused, but neither was he accepted off-hand.

In the interval between the proposal and the answer, he was forestalled by his friend Count Reuss, who was more favorably received, and to whom his cousin was soon afterwards married. The disappointment does not appear to have been a heartbreaking one. And the young man seems to have submitted to it with equal philosophy and piety. It is a curious episode in his life, but one that need not further be pursued.

On May 26th, 1721, the Count attained his majority, and soon after, he returned to Hennersdorf. He had finished his education and his travels, and a new kind of life was about to begin.

The two years which had elapsed had been of the greatest importance. He had seen the world, and had been preserved from the world. He had neither been dazzled by its false splendors, nor deceived by its "lying delights." He had learnt to know by closer observation the various churches. In all of them he had met with true disciples of Jesus Christ.

"All of us, however numerous and however various we are," said Luther, "all of us who have been washed in the blood of Christ are the true Church; we are all members of Christ, and are all brethren, whether we belong to Rome or Wittenberg or Jerusalem."

This great principle, the true Protestant principle, had been strangely lost sight of since Luther's day, and at the beginning of the eighteenth century it would have sounded like a heresy. It was reserved to Zinzendorf to bring it to the light again, and he could do this better than most men, for with him it was not merely a theoretical principle, it was a practical experience.

Finally, Zinzendorf had been initiated into suffering and sacrifice. His sympathetic soul had often been misunderstood. His own family very imperfectly comprehended the need for holiness and devotion to the Savior, which formed the basis of his being. Moreover, along with the need for activity which consumed him, he had felt a certain lassitude, as we may gather from a letter to a friend, in which he touchingly beseeches him to ask God to lead him like a little child, and with the cords of love; "and pray," says he, "that I may find a little corner where for a moment I may lay aside my pilgrim's staff."

Chapter 8

Life at Court

After eleven years' absence Zinzendorf now found himself in the place where he had spent his earliest days. Young and full of imagination, trained by his travels for commerce with the world, rich in knowledge and experience, he found at Hennersdorf none but the rather monotonous society of three old ladies—his grandmother, the Baroness; Madame de Mensbach, his great aunt; and his aunt, Mlle. de Gersdorf. We see him, however, engaged in congenial occupation, devoting his time to the religious education of two boys, and presiding at public meetings in the castle for purposes of edification.

But the time was now come for him to choose a career, or rather to enter on the career which his grandmother and his aunts, who continued to treat him as a child, had chosen for him. They had decided that he should enter the service of the king, in a civil and political capacity. Had Zinzendorf been consulted, his choice would not have been doubtful. He thought there was nothing so delightful as to preach the Gospel. The study of theology and the humble position of a pastor was the sole object of his ambition.

From his childhood he had felt himself called to lead souls to Christ, and this desire had deepened with his years. He therefore besought his relatives to allow him to obey this inward call. But, in spite of his prayers and tears, they would not consent to his thus demeaning himself. The good ladies, with all their pietism, could not conceive that a man with good sense could wish to be a minister of Jesus Christ when he might be the minister of the King of Poland.

Zinzendorf, as usual, submitted to the will of his relatives:

> I know that self-will may easily be mixed with our projects when we oppose the express will of our parents and guardians. I therefore enter the service of the State, so long as they take it upon

> themselves to command me. This is what I call the vocation of obedience. If I resisted at first, it was not from pride or stubbornness, but from very different motives, and I do not doubt that the God Who sends me to Dresden against my inclinations will richly bless me. And yet, however little I may understand the directions of God, it is impossible for me not to conclude that He has really predestined me to be a laborer in the Church of Brotherly Love.

These last words are very noteworthy. There is something prophetic in this vision. One cannot but admire this deep sense of vocation at the moment when everything seemed to contradict it. *And yet!* It is the word of Galilee. It is the protest of all great souls. It is the cry of faith.

It was towards the end of 1721 that Zinzendorf entered on his duties in the Government of the Electorate of Saxony. During the five years that he spent in office, his duties were confined to settling disputes between a few peasants and their lord. He had intimated to the Chancellor at the outset that he had no desire for advancement, and had begged to be charged with this kind of business.

Careless of worldly success, preoccupied with spiritual interests, Zinzendorf gave umbrage to no one, and in return they overlooked any little eccentricities in his piety, and any excess in his zeal. He says:

> I arrived at court. My parents wished it, and I could not get out of it. What was I to do? I wished to conserve my treasure. I wished to be the friend of God and the enemy of the world. And so I began with well-meant impertinences, which now, as I think of them, I cannot too much admire the patience and politeness of all the members of the court and of the ministry, whom I must have wearied with my devotions.

Chapter 9

Marriage and Settlement at Berthelsdorf

Since the early days of Pietism, the religious situation in Germany has been sensibly modified. Pietism, at first despised and persecuted, had become fashionable among the higher classes of society. It had become the proper thing to take the side of the Halle professors, and the clergy had at length arrived at the conclusion that men who were in so high repute at court could not be altogether in the wrong.

The Wittenberg theology lost ground. But, as all men know, it is through victory after victory that a party comes to ruin, and this was the case with the Pietists. They lost in real life what they gained in power and consideration, while the orthodox, tempered by disgrace, learnt, in their turn, to live by faith. All this was, for Zinzendorf, a new lesson in impartiality. Brought up by the Pietists, he had always, in spite of them, been regarded as one of them. But from this time he ceased to carry the colors of a party, and extended his sympathies, more and more, to all Christians without distinction. This made him many enemies.

All this time, also, many were feeling the need of a new reformation in the Protestant Churches. They had a general impression that the work of Luther had been left unfinished, that the German Churches that had sprung from the religious movement of the sixteenth century had not been constituted entirely according to the principles of the Gospel, and that, in matters of ecclesiastical discipline especially, there was much to be desired.

Zinzendorf shared this feeling, and it was not until some years afterwards that he ceased to interest himself in this kind of questions. Only, he did not feel himself called to spend his strength on what he considered, even then, to be secondary matters, and he saw clearly what risk men run in paying so much attention to forms, of losing sight of the one thing truly needful. His constant and unique desire was to discover the true friends of the Savior in every church, and to help them to "keep the unity of the Spirit in the bond of peace."

To this end he longed to have a home of his own in which he might offer a refuge to all sorts of Christians, and especially to those who might be persecuted and oppressed. He therefore purchased from his grandmother the estate of Berthelsdorf, close to her residence. He did not quit his charge at Dresden, but he devoted himself principally to the happiness of his new vassals, and to the promotion among them of that spirit of brotherly love which he had so much at heart.

The cure of Berthelsdorf had just become vacant, and the nomination of a pastor was the first administrative act that Zinzendorf had to perform. It will easily be understood what importance this duty assumed in his eyes and with what scrupulous care he discharged it. He decided to call to this charge the candidate Rothe, a fervent Christian and a distinguished preacher, whom certain conscientious scruples had hitherto kept without a church. Rothe accepted, and Zinzendorf, accepting the position of a deacon, set himself to second the pastor's efforts by every means in his power.

Having provided for the spiritual needs of his tennants, the new lord occupied himself with his own arrangements. He entrusted the administration of his domains to his aunt's old steward, Heitz, whom he had brought from Oberberg. As the owners of Berthelsdorf had not lived in it for upwards of two hundred years, the mansion was uninhabitable. Zinzendorf, therefore, was obliged to build himself a house. It was to be a very simple structure, as those who were to live in it were merely sojourners, whose real home was in Heaven.

He wished also to take to himself a helpmeet who should second him in his work, and he believed he had found one in one of the sisters of his friend Count Reuss, whose name was Ermuth Dorothea, and whose acquaintance he had made at Ebersdorf. He had often inclined to celibacy, which at times had appeared to be more conformed to his ideal of holiness. But his experience of the world had taught him how much risk is run by those who place themselves outside the normal conditions of existence.

"I am young," he wrote to Cardinal de Noailles, "but my hair grows white with fear when I see my soul, the spouse of Christ, exposed to so many perils from the flesh and from the lightness of our nature." Moreover, he recognized in marriage a Divine institution, a type of the union between Christ and the soul, and hence a means of sanctification. Concerning his projected union he wrote as follows to his grandmother:

> There are other difficulties, for I am a strange mortal, and I admit that the Countess will have to be content to live with me a life of renunciation. Like me, she will have to throw to the winds all chimeras of rank and quality, for these things are not established by God, but are invented by the vanity of man. If she wishes to be useful to me, she will also have to employ herself in that which is essential to my life, by helping me to win men to Christ, and this in the midst of opprobrium and contempt.

Nor did the Count hide these things from his intended bride. He frankly declared that he did not wish to live for himself, but for his neighbor and for God; that he was disgusted with the vanities of the world; that he did not propose to please men; and that, finally, he was ready if God called him to it, to take his staff in his hand and go and preach to the heathen. And, in order at once to release himself from whatever might hinder him in his work, he renounced all his earthly goods by means of a deed of gift, to his future wife.

We shall see, further on, the important part that the Countess took in all the works of her husband. He himself paid a high tribute to her in a page of his *Natural Reflections,* written in 1747: "An experience of a quarter of a century has taught me that the helpmeet I have is the only one in all respects suited to my vocation." The marriage was celebrated in the month of September at Ebersdorf, and shortly afterwards the Count and Countess settled at Dresden.

Chapter 10

The Moravian Immigrants—Foundation of Herrnhut

The prayers of Zinzendorf were about to be answered. In his absence, God prepared for him and as it were, without him, the work to which he was destined. The hand of the Lord brought out of Egypt, and transplanted on the slopes of Berthelsdorf, the chosen vine which He designed to place beneath His servant's care.

As, from this moment, the history of Zinzendorf and that of the Unity of Moravian Brethren become inseparably intertwined, it will be well briefly to recall the previous development of that ancient Church, which was about to be revived under a new form and with another constitution. In order to do this it will not be necessary to tell the wonderful story from the beginning.

From the ninth to the eighteenth century, it is one long story of persecution and endurance and triumph. At the beginning of the latter century a spirit of emigration arose in Bohemia and Moravia, and many members of the Church of the Brethren, feeling that it was in vain to look for liberty of conscience in their native land, began to turn their feet towards Western Europe.

The man whom Providence raised up to lead this movement in its origin was a Moravian carpenter named Christian David. He was, according to his contemporaries, a man of uncommon energy and capacity. Born and brought up in the Roman Church, he had from his childhood been the subject of religious impressions. Leaving his native country very early in life, he had followed his trade in various towns in Germany. The reading of the Bible had brought him to Christ, and he had joined the Lutheran Church. He had afterwards returned to Moravia on several occasions and become connected with many members of the community of Brethren. Through him, a revival had taken place among them, and a clearer knowledge of the Gospel and a more living faith had strengthened their traditional attachment to the doctrine of their fathers. They also groaned more deeply beneath the oppression they had to bear.

At the beginning of 1722, David found himself in Lusatia, where he met with Zinzendorf, and was introduced to him. He pictured with great vivacity the miserable condition of his co-religionists in Moravia, and incidentally commended to the protection of the Count those of them who had decided to emigrate. The Count did not think much of what he had heard, though he had listened to the story with interest; but the carpenter had seen into the soul of Zinzendorf, and started for Moravia, where, on his arrival, he spoke with enthusiasm of what he had seen.

There was at that time in the village at Sehlen, in Moravia, a family of five brethren. They were born Catholics, but their maternal grandfather, a descendant of the ancient Bohemian Church, had instructed them in the doctrines of Scripture. The pious conversations of an Imperial soldier had recently awakened in them the impressions of their childhood, and they had secretly resolved to leave all they possessed, and go to some country where they and their children might safely seek the salvation of their souls.

They thought first of Hungary, but they were not satisfied with the result of their inquiries. On hearing the report of David, and on his advice, they decided to seek refuge in Lusatia. Two of them, famous artisans —"the famous cutlers," Zinzendorf called them—resolved to start without delay. Abandoning their houses and their goods, they set forth secretly with their wives and little ones, under the guidance of the brave carpenter. They reached Berthelsdorf in the month of June. The Count was not at home, but they had letters of recommendation for the steward, Heitz, and for Marche, the tutor of the grandchildren of the Baroness Gersdorf.

Heitz wrote to Zinzendorf to inform him of the arrival of the little party. Zinzendorf, who was on the eve of his marriage, wrote in haste to say that they might stay on his estate until better provision could be found for them. He intended to obtain permission from Count Reuss to settle them on his land. He did not know that these poor people were to be the firstfruits of that Community of Brotherly Love of which he had so often dreamed, and which the Lord was beginning to gather around him.

But in the absence of the Count the affair took an unexpected turn. The Baroness became interested in the newcomers. She sent them a cow to supply their little ones with milk, and permitted them to cut wood in the forest for a house. This house was to be built on the Count's land near the main road to Zittau. It was a piece of waste ground at the foot of a little hill called the Houtberg.

It was on the 17th of June, 1722, that they set to work—a memorable day in the annals of the Church of the Brethren; for the cottage that was then begun was the first house of the future town of Herrnhut. Christian David, striking his axe into a pine tree, exclaimed: "Here the sparrow hath found an house, and the swallow a nest for herself, even Thine altars, O Lord of hosts!"

The building presented many difficulties, but they worked with courage, and each one seemed to feel that a special blessing must attend an enterprise begun in faith. In the sermon preached at the installation of Pastor Rothe by his friend Schœfer we find the following prophetic words: "God will kindle on these hills a light which will shine in every land; I am sure of it by faith." The axe of Christian David struck the first spark.

In the end of December the Count and Countess Zinzendorf, returning to pass the winter on their estates, drove along the road which runs from the little village of Strahwald to the castle of Hennersdorf. Night had already fallen. In the woods at the foot of the Houtberg the Count perceived an unwonted light. He enquired what it was, and was told that it was the dwelling of the Moravian emigrants.

The Lord had prepared for him that recompense. He had proved himself faithful in that which had been entrusted to him thus far; a greater and a more important work was now to be committed to his care. He quickly alighted, and entering the house where his new guests were seated round their peaceful hearth, he warmly bade them welcome. Then kneeling down with them, he solemnly gave thanks to God, and asked His blessing on the house that they had built, and on all who dwelt therein.

Chapter 11

Three Friends of Zinzendorf

The Count and Countess did not arrive alone. Frederick de Watteville had joined them at Dresden, and traveled with them. This college friend of Zinzendorf was now to be his fellow-worker. God permitted the two young men to realize together the pious designs that had filled their childish imaginations.

Schrautenbach, who knew Watteville personally, has left us a most interesting portrait of him. He was, according to Schrautenbach, a noble character, quite above suspicion, and inspiring confidence even in men who had lost all faith in human nature; without pretension, unaffected, affable; of a proved fidelity and thoroughly devoted to his brethren; humble, charitable, carefully seeking out the good points in every one; of great penetration; a man of great energy and endurance. He was temperamental, forgetful, absent-minded and yet with the education, the appearance, and the manners of a gentleman.

Such was the man whom God had chosen to be the Melanchthon of Zinzendorf, and one of the pillars of the new Church of the Brethren. But, at the period of which we are speaking, he had not found peace to his soul. His development had not the regularity which we admire in the Count. Since leaving college Watteville had spent most of his time in Paris. He had seen the world and loved it. Carried away, like most others, by the fury of speculation, he had won and lost enormous sums of money. Philosophy, also, had fascinated him, and had insensibly robbed him of the simple faith in which he had been reared.

But neither the wisdom nor the folly of the world had succeeded in satisfying that choice spirit. Disgusted betimes by its lying vanities, he essayed to find again the peace and joy of his early years, by placing himself once more under the beneficent influence of a friend who had inspired him with as much confidence as respect.

During the early days of his residence at Hennersdorf and Berthelsdorf, his heart was still divided. In religious meetings he was the subject of lively emotions, but he was not entirely detached from the world. The severe inhabitants of the castle at Hennersdorf felt that he was not one of them. He was therefore in little request, and had ample time for reflection. A great work was going on within him. The Count, who loved him tenderly, did not seek to hurry his conversion. He respected the delicacy of his nature, and confined himself to praying for him and encouraging him.

One evening, however, about a month after their arrival, seeing him unusually sad, Zinzendorf spoke to him and enquired after his spiritual condition. Watteville told him that his soul was in a frightful state of chaos, and that he was as miserable as it was possible to be. "What idea hast thou formed of God?" asked the Count. Watteville enumerated the perfections that he attributed to the Divine Being, but dared not speak of His love. Whereupon Zinzendorf dwelt upon this great quality as being of the very essence of the Deity, and sang to him some hymns setting forth the love of the Savior or depicting the misery of man. Watteville threw himself upon his knees imploring the Divine mercy, and besought God to say to his soul: "Let there be light."

Little by little light came, and we shall soon reach the decisive moment when the young man devoted himself entirely to the service of the Savior. The bonds of friendship with the Count became now closer than ever. Two other men shared their intimacy—Rothe the pastor, and Schrefer of Grerlitz, whom Rothe had introduced to them. Schoefer was a faithful minister of Christ, and he had already suffered much for his Master.

Rothe, Schoefer, Watteville, and Zinzendorf then formed one of those little private associations that the Count so dearly loved, whose object was to attack the kingdom of darkness, and to extend the kingdom of Christ. The means that commended themselves to them were the preaching of the Gospel, in the demonstration of the Spirit, and with a direct view to the conversion of souls; the foundation of Christian educational establishments; the publication and dissemination of useful, edifying books; and, finally, frequent intercourse with Christians of various countries by means of travel and of correspondence.

The four friends had frequent friendly conferences. Rothe brought to them a rare, persuasive eloquence, his systematic mind, his profound knowledge of Scripture; Schoefer, his vivacity, his bold and enterprising spirit, his knowledge of the human heart, his almost excessive frankness; Watteville, his clear and penetrating intellect, his direct and unembellished style of speech, and his attractive character. Zinzendorf, by his ardent love for the Savior and his genius for organization, was the soul of the association.

In things indifferent, he readily subordinated his opinion to that of his friends; but, once he was convinced that it was founded on the Bible, nothing could shake him. It was Zinzendorf that took charge of the correspondence, and composed the literature of the society. He also set up a printing press and issued cheap editions of the Psalms and other manuals of devotion, and eventually of the whole Bible. Nor did he neglect the more specific duties of the diaconate or the more direct and personal efforts to which he had been accustomed for the salvation of souls.

This is how the Sunday was passed at Berthelsdorf. After sermon and catechism, the pastor and his flock assembled in church, talked over the subjects that had been treated, each one freely expressing his ideas and asking questions or starting objections, as the case might be. Prayer followed conversation; after which the Count, accompanied on the organ by Tobias Friedrich, one of the men-servants, edified the audience by singing psalms and hymns and spiritual songs. These psalms were often improvised, and, as many will believe, inspired.

At a later period the Brethren began to collect them as they were produced, and many of them are preserved in their Psalmody. In the afternoon, the parishioners used to meet in the Castle, and the Count would repeat and comment on the sermon they had heard in the morning.

Chapter 12

Development of the Colony

After a short tour in Silesia, Zinzendorf returned to Dresden, leaving on his estates his friend Watteville, who had taken to heart the interests of the Moravian emigrants. These continued to increase. Three new houses had been added to the first. The Count had determined to erect a boarding-house at Herrnhut for their special benefit. This is what was afterwards known as the Common House.

Baron Watteville did not reside in either of the castles of his friends. Man of the world as he was by his training and by the elegance of his manners, he loved solitude and the company of common people. He had therefore taken up his lodgings in a little chamber in one of the houses on the Houtberg.

Early one morning he was awakened by the other inmates of the house who had risen to go to their work, and he heard them at their family prayers. The partitions were thin, and he overheard these poor people pouring out their hearts to God. He was deeply moved—so deeply that he himself began to pray with fervor and with importunity. He went out of doors, and walked to the timberyard of Christian David, and there, seated on a log of wood, he reviewed his whole life, and reflected on the chain of circumstances that, apart from his own will, had brought him into the midst of these people.

The result was a solemn resolution to consecrate himself entirely and forever to God and to the work He had given him to do. He was so absorbed in his thoughts that he did not notice what was passing, when he was aroused by the voice of the carpenter who had just finished a piece of work: "There, at last it is done, and we shall be able to lay the first stone of the new house today."

"And I also," answered the Baron, "I am ready and I will help you."

The same evening, the stone was solemnly laid by Zinzendorf, who had recently arrived from Dresden. It was for Watteville a time of decision. He was still under the sway of the morning's emotions. He had placed under the foundation stone his rings and other jewelry—everything that seemed to bind him to a worldly life. After the discourse of the Count, he knelt upon the stone and poured out his soul in a prayer which expressed all his resolutions, all his desires and hopes, and which moved and melted all the standers-by. Zinzendorf often declared that he had never heard anything like it, and to this prayer he was accustomed to trace the rich outpouring of grace which almost immediately followed.

On this same day—May 12th, 1724—a new batch of emigrants had arrived at Herrnhut. The revival brought about in Moravia by Christian David continued to spread: two whole villages had been moved by the breath of the Holy Spirit. Among the newcomers was another carpenter, of the name of David Nitschmann, who afterwards became the first bishop of the new Church.

In the course of five years the number of emigrants increased to three hundred, and the number of houses on the Houtberg to thirty. During that period many disastrous differences arose between the various members of the little community, owing largely to the ignorance and fanaticism of some of the later immigrants, and to the diversity of ecclesiastical taste and opinion that existed in the colony.

These troubles, and particularly the defection of Christian David, were a source of constant trial to the Count, but through them all he firmly kept the faith and steadfastly maintained his hope in God. Nor was he disappointed. Towards the end of 1726, the way was opened by the death of his grandmother, and by the reluctant connivance of his mother, for his retirement from his charge at court, and he was enabled to devote himself exclusively to the work on which his heart was set.

Chapter 13

The Community Enlarged and Organized

A new period in the life of Zinzendorf opens from the moment of his leaving Dresden and settling on his estates. From that moment, Herrnhut becomes the exclusive object of his care. His one business is to labor for the temporal and spiritual good of the new colony. Nothing could be more disinterested than his efforts, for the hospitality he extended to these poor people cost him dear, and he had no honors to expect from it. Indeed, his liberality, from the first, brought him nothing but scandal from the world, which condemned him in order that it might dispense with admiring him.

In order that he might devote himself wholly to his task, he committed the administration of his temporal affairs to his wife and to his friend Watteville. Seeing also that his daily journeys to Herrnhut took up too much time, he quitted the house he had built at Berthelsdorf, and lodged in an unfinished wing of the great house at the foot of the Houtberg.

The crisis through which the community was passing called for all the zeal of Zinzendorf, but did not cause him undue anxiety. As he had foreseen, he was able speedily to bring back into the Evangelical Church those who had been alienated from it. Patience and charity, the power of the Spirit and the Word of God—these were his weapons. But while readily returning from their sectarian tendencies, the Moravians of Herrnhut did not the less persist in claiming the re-establishment of the ancient constitution of their Church. They would listen to nothing which threatened to turn them from it, and they plainly told the Count that nothing would ever shake their resolution. It was well known, they said, that what the other churches needed was an organization of this kind. Luther himself had admitted that. On this point, the Brethren had a marked advantage.

And, in the last resort, they declared that, much as they should regret it, if the constitution was not granted, they would be obliged to leave Herrnhut and seek a refuge elsewhere.

Zinzendorf was well aware of the embarrassments into which he would enter by granting their request. Nevertheless he felt bound carefully to examine it. "I see," said he, "that it is necessary either to abandon these poor erring lambs to fanaticism or to restore their ecclesiastical organization."

He consulted many persons, and carefully studied Comenius on *The History of the Brethren.* He comments:

> When I came to the end of the book, my mind was made up, and I said: "Yes, I will labor to restore it. Body and goods, honor and life, I will risk all for this. So long as I live, and if possible after I am gone, this little flock which belongs to the Savior shall be preserved for Him until He comes again."

Zinzendorf set himself to work, and in consultation with Rothe and some of the principal inhabitants of Herrnhut, drew up a number of statutes in conformity with the practices of the Apostolic Churches and the ancient constitution of the Brethren, so far as they were suited to present circumstances. He then called together the whole community and spoke to them for three hours under deep emotion, and, at the close, he read to them the articles proposed.

The first of them was as follows:

> "The members of the community at Herrnhut should have a constant love to their brethren, the children of God of every religion. They ought to permit neither judgment, nor blame, nor inconsiderate word against those who think differently from them, but they ought to see to it that they preserve amongst themselves the purity of the Gospel, simplicity, and grace."

The statutes were unanimously adopted. Each one signed them and engaged to keep them. All of them expressed their penitence at having allowed themselves to be misled into useless squabbles. They declared they would abandon them for ever, and that, for the future, they would seek to be poor in spirit and allow themselves to be guided by the Holy Ghost. In short, there was at that moment a powerful effusion of grace that moved and subjugated every heart.

This took place on the 12th of May, 1727. Three years before, they had laid the first stone of the Common House. The faith and love which then had filled all hearts had been restored. The Holy Spirit continued to breathe upon them and to brood over the emerging community with creative energy. Scarcely a day passed on which some new institution did not spring forth to sanction and consolidate the recent union of hearts and to complete the edifice of the growing Church.

One Sunday, for example, Rothe and other ministers had preached on the same subject simultaneously, in three or four places. This subject, which was taken from the Gospel for the day, was the visit of the Virgin to Elizabeth. They had dwelt upon the advantages of Christian friendship and communion, provided always that when Christians meet, the Savior is in the midst of them. The result of the sermons was to create a general desire for Christian fellowship. Little associations were formed of two, three, or four persons who met together for mutual confession of faults, and for spiritual conversation and prayer.

In less than eight days, under the guidance of Zinzendorf, the whole parish was grouped into these little companies. They called them "bands." These bands were always composed of persons of the same sex, and according to their different degrees of spiritual development. The heads of the community often rearranged them lest the Church should become split up into little groups that might become strangers to each other. The influence of these bands was immense. Without them, Zinzendorf often declared, Herrnhut would never have become what it was.

A still more important institution was that of "choirs." In these larger groups, the members were arranged according to age, and sex, and civil status. There was the choir of married men, of bachelors, of boys, of infants, of widows, of married women, of maidens, etc. In each of these classes, certain members, designated "workers," were charged with a sort of ministry. Each choir also had separate meetings for edification, a separate psalmody, and separate days of festival.

Luxury was carefully banished from the toilet of the women. All finery and jewelry were forbidden. Even fans and parasols were banned. A very simple little hat, or more commonly, a white bonnet without lace, tied on with a bit of ribbon, composed their headdress. The color of the ribbon served to distinguish the sisters belonging to the different choirs: white for widows, blue for matrons, pink for maidens, red for younger girls.

For the men there were no distinguishing marks, but all were plainly dressed, mostly in grey or brown. Mourning was never worn, for they considered death a "departure" or "returning home," not a subject of grief.

They also organized a night watch, all the men from 16 to 60 taking part in it by turns. The object was not so much security as to "mount guard" before the Eternal. (This was the meaning of the name Herrnhut, the Lord's watch or guard.) The watch announced the time by chanting a verse appropriate to each hour of the night and destined to lift the thoughts of those who were still awake to the Lord.

A few brethren and sisters established, in addition, what they called "a round of prayer." They distributed the twenty-four hours of each day amongst themselves, and engaged to consecrate them all and fill them up with prayer for all. This prayer at first took the form of intercession for the whole Church of Christ, and in particular for Herrnhut. They afterwards added to it a special prayer for the divers communities of the Brethren, for the different choirs, for missionaries, ministers, evangelists, the public authorities, etc. It was the perpetual offering. It was, according to the word of Isaiah, the watchmen set on the walls of Jerusalem, and not holding their peace day or night.

These institutions, although regulated by Zinzendorf, were, for the most part, the spontaneous offspring of the new life which had begun to flow through all the veins of the community. It was, in fact, a time of grace, a time of refreshing from the presence of the Lord to solace them after so many trials and to prepare them for further conflicts.

The 13th of August, 1727, stands out among these blessed days: it is the day that is still observed as the real foundation of the New Moravian Brotherhood. No great external event has marked it out. The Holy Spirit on that day filled the whole community. They had gone to Berthelsdorf, at the invitation of the pastor, Rothe, to celebrate the Holy Supper at the parish church. During Divine Service, and especially during the Communion, all who were there experienced, in an indescribable manner, the presence of the Savior in the midst of them.

It was, for all of them, a Pentecost. By this baptism of the Spirit, God witnessed His approval of the new community, and expressed His pleasure in it. "From that day." says David Nitschmann, "Herrnhut became a living Church of Jesus Christ. On it the Brethren renewed their solemn vows to serve the Lord at all times, everywhere, in all ways, at all costs and risks.... In a word, we were lifted out of ourselves, and young and old began a new and heavenly life."

But the greater the enthusiasm, the more urgent was the necessity of maintaining purity of doctrine and simplicity of faith. Zinzendorf also continued to devote all his attention to the preaching of the Word. In one of his works, composed at that time, and entitled, *Considerations on the Work of a Preacher,* we see in what manner he regarded this function. It is addressed to a theologian:

> I will tell you quite simply how I proceed when I have to preach. I presume at the outset that the soul should be occupied exclusively with the things of God: that the mouth ought to speak out of the abundance of the heart: that God has promised His servants that it shall not be they who speak, but the Spirit of their Father Who is in them. Moreover, I should never begin to speak without first reflecting on my own impotence, and looking down into the gulf of human misery and into the abysses of the love of God in Jesus Christ. This makes us careful not to speak our own thoughts merely, and makes us happy in the privilege of proclaiming the great fact of reconciliation.
>
> As to the subject of discourse, what can this be but the mystery of redemption and the mystery of salvation? These two points ought to be presented with seriousness and affection. Only that which directly affects the souls of the hearers should be presented. It is less the arguments of the intellect than the emotions of the heart of the preacher which affect and move them.

It was not the explanation of Scripture that most preoccupied the Count. This, he thought, required a special gift which he had not received. He writes in 1735:

> During the eight years that I labored in the Church as a lay catechist, I never attempted expressly to interpret the Scriptures—

> that is to say, to positively declare that an apostle or a prophet meant to say such and such a thing when the matter was not so clear that everyone, whether a Christian or not, would understand it in the same sense. I confined myself, therefore, to well-known and incontestable truths, and this has always succeeded best with me. Indeed, although I was well aware that knowledge is not the essential thing, and although I had learnt fairly well to distinguish in theological principles those which are certain from those which are probable, and from those which are corollaries from both, I was, nevertheless, exceedingly afraid of falling into the slightest error, for I knew what influence it might have upon the will.
>
> Moreover, I regarded it as an extreme happiness not to fall into error myself or to lead others astray. By the grace of God, and by keeping to essential and fundamental and clearly and repeatedly revealed truths, this is not as difficult as one might suppose.

From this it will be seen what Zinzendorf's method was. One would hardly have expected to find such prudence and wisdom in a man so young, and so full of imagination and of such fervent piety. It will also be seen what, at that time, was his doctrine. It was the doctrine of grace and salvation by Jesus Christ, the dogma of all the churches, the commonplace of all confessions of faith, which, nevertheless, always keeps the freshness of paradox and appears to be a novelty every time it is announced anew.

Zinzendorf did not content himself with the stated preaching of the Gospel. He loved to seize all solemn occasions to bear witness to the truths of salvation. Thus, every time Rothe conducted a baptism, a wedding, or a funeral, the Count added some words of exhortation, to impress upon the audience the seriousness of the ceremony, and to urge upon them the duties incumbent on them. Frequently he gave readings in public—now a portion of Scripture or of some religious treatise, now a letter containing news of interest to the kingdom of God.

In this way, in 1727, he gave to his friends a large part of an abridgment that he had made of the *History of the Brethren of Bohemia, Poland,* and *Moravia,* by Comenius. He had such a gift for reading that the very accent of his words threw a flood of light on the most obscure passages, and added a charm to that which was quite clear.

He also attached great importance to the singing of psalms as a means of edification, and with the help of his secretary, Tobias Friedrich, who was an excellent musician, he organized singing classes and choirs. His memory for psalms was not less remarkable than his powers of improvisation. He would often sing a series of verses borrowed from various psalms or joined together by means of verses of his own composed upon the spot. Of all these fragments he made up a sort of chanted discourse, and those who heard him bore witness to the profound impression produced by this lyrical preaching. It was like an echo of the ancient dithyrambs (impassioned utterances) of the prophets of Israel. *Agapes* or love feasts, such as were celebrated by the early Christians, were also held.

Nor did the interest he took in the spiritual development of his tennants cause the Count to overlook their material wellbeing. He felt for them with a father's heart, and concerned himself in everything that might improve their condition. It was no easy matter to secure a livelihood for a population of emigrants, most of whom were penniless and easily carried away by their religious feelings to a life of contemplation, and, by their blind faith, to an easy, careless *laissez-faire.*

The revenues of Zinzendorf would not have been sufficient to maintain them, even if he had not regarded labor as the first and foremost duty of man. He therefore set himself to find employment for them according to their capacities, and put them in the way of self-support. He did not abandon his seignorial authority. On the contrary, he gave to his bailiff at Berthelsdorf full powers of police. At the same time, he invited the Brethren to bring their differences before arbitrators chosen from among themselves. These arbitrators formed a "communal tribunal."

Other Brethren were charged with the distribution of alms, and with the care of the sick; while still others constituted a sort of labor bureau, whose functions were to find employment and to see that the work was well done and sold at a reasonable price. Inspectors also were appointed to detect incipient abuses, and it was their duty to report immediately to other servants of the Church, whose special function was fraternally to warn those whose conduct might give rise to reproach.

Similar constitutions often display very little knowledge of men, and fail from want of wisdom in the working of them. In this case, we cannot but admire both the adaptation of the institutions to the needs of the community and the skill with which they were administered. Zinzendorf showed consummate knowledge and consummate ability both in shaping the constitution of Herrnhut and in working it so that the government should neither degenerate into despotism nor encourage that license which would have fatally hindered the development of the common life of the society. But there was something more than wisdom here, there was the working of the very Spirit of life.

The education of children also received much attention. The college for young nobles was replaced by an orphanage. When Zinzendorf endeavored to move the children by speaking to them of the sufferings of the Savior, however, he was much discouraged by what he thought was their hardness and indifference, but he consoled himself with the thought that Jesus loved the little ones. He gave himself to prayer for them, and soon his prayers were answered. A very beautiful work of grace broke out amongst them, and he had the joy of seeing little groups of them, of their own accord, leaving their homes and wending their way to the heights of the Houtberg to pray together. The Count followed them at a distance, and kept watch over them to see that they were not disturbed. Then, when they came down the hill he would join them, and, uniting his voice with theirs, he would march into the village with them chanting the praises of God. Zinzendorf comments:

> The true method of Christian education is to speak to their souls from their infancy, in order to teach them one thing; that they belong to Jesus, and that their happiness consists in knowing Him, possessing Him, serving Him, living with Him, and that their greatest misery would be to be separated from Him in any way.

In these ways had the Count attained the end he aimed at in settling down at Herrnhut. All divisions had been healed; the community of the Brethren had been born again; the prayer of Comenius had been answered, and Zinzendorf had been chosen of God to build again the ruins of the old Moravian Church.

Chapter 14

Visit to Jena and Halle

The time had now come when Herrnhut was to enter into contact with the outside world. In this matter it was again the zeal and enterprise of Zinzendorf which determined the destinies of the new community. If he had been content merely to preside over the little Moravian Church, if he had limited his activities to that narrow sphere, it is probable that the community would not long have survived him. But the Count was not the man to circumscribe his work. If duty has limits, love has none.

Zinzendorf recognized that Herrnhut had the first claim upon him, but not by any means the only claim. He did not belong to Herrnhut, but to the Lord, and he was ready to go wherever the Master sent him. "The love of Christ constrained him" to tell out in every place the grace by which he lived.

In the midst of the exacting toil to which he had given himself, therefore, in the way of organization and oversight at home, he made frequent journeys in the year 1727 of an evangelistic kind to other places, and sent deputations into other lands. John and David Nitschmann were sent to Denmark, and another "messenger" to England in the following year. Zinzendorf's chief visits were paid to Jena, where the students at the university and the trades-people flocked to hear him; and to Halle, where he had been invited by his friends. At Halle he preached in the Pœdagogium, from the words, "I thank Thee, O Father, Lord of Heaven and earth, because Thou hast hid these from the wise and prudent and hast revealed them unto babes."

The sensation produced by his presence and by his preaching in both these illustrious universities, was immense. It attracted to him the eyes of all the theological and religious world in Germany. "It excited the enthusiasm of some, the distrust of others, the attention of all."

The absence of the Count from Herrnhut, however, though it only lasted three months, had a most injurious effect. No sooner had he left, than the faith of many grew weak. Many of the members began to quake for the stability of their little church, formed in haste, without any recognized existence, and without official connection with other Evangelical Churches. This equivocal position might, they thought, expose them to grave embarrassments and even to persecution, and they began to ask whether, after all, it would not be best to renounce the name and the traditions of the Brethren, and settle down in the Lutheran Church. This tendency was manifesting itself among many influential members of the community. Rothe, who appears never to have fully entered into the views of Zinzendorf, was one of the first to give way to it, and Christian David followed suit.

The Count was still at Jena when he received the news. It will be remembered that, at the outset, these were the Count's own views, and that he had only abandoned them in consequence of the formal and determined opposition that they had met with from the Brethren. But now, he could not see without displeasure and concern the levity with which they were prepared to pull down that which had just been built, and to abandon institutions which had already begun to bear such good fruit, and on which the blessing of God had rested in a manner so marked. He foresaw that the proposed new departure would inevitably lead to a schism in the community, for he knew that there were many of the Brethren that would never raise their hand for this new resolution.

But what grieved him most were the considerations that had given rise to the project. It seemed to him unworthy of a Christian community to let itself be influenced by the fear of the sufferings to which they might be exposed, and to renounce, from a motive so miserable, a liberty which their ancestors had conquered by their blood.

On his return, however, he managed, by great tact, and after much persuasion, to allay the agitation, and a great love-feast crowned and sealed the work of union and of peace.

Chapter 15

Further Development of the Community

The crisis through which the community had passed, as is always the case where there is real life, was the occasion of further progress and development. Zinzendorf redoubled his vigilance, and set himself to adapt his teaching to the needs of his hearers. He urged upon them the exhortation of St. Peter, to "add to their faith virtue," in order that they might not be "barren or unfruitful in the knowledge of Christ," but "make their calling and election sure." He gave them a series of lectures on "the fruits of the Spirit." For this purpose he took for his text the saying of St. Paul, "And now abideth faith, hope, charity," and to these virtues he reduced all the others, joining to faith prayer, vigilance, and patience; to charity gentleness, humility, benignity; and to hope temperance, contentment, prudence, etc.

Desiring scrupulously to conform to all the precepts of the Savior, he did not scruple to introduce into his household a practice that is neglected by Protestants—the washing of feet. He saw in the words of the Lord (John 13:14, 15) a positive precept. It was not until later, at Herrnhaag, that the ceremony was introduced into public worship. It was then performed before the Lord's Supper. The Church of the Brethren did not abolish it until 1818.

By degrees, also, the various practices of the community were more minutely regulated. The Lord's Supper was celebrated every month, and every month a solemn day for prayer and praise was set apart. A manual and guide to intercession was prepared, containing the names and particulars of the condition of the various persons and interests to be brought before the Lord. And, most difficult and delicate task of all, a code of discipline and a form of excommunication were drawn up.

The practical sense of the Count led him to see that, if the direction of the affairs of the Church was to be maintained in vigor and efficiency, it must not always remain in the same hands. New forces began to manifest themselves; new blood was made; many young men of zeal and intelligence sprang up. Desiring, therefore, to bring about a general re-election of officers, he himself resigned the presidency in 1730. The elders followed his example, and were at once replaced, but the presidency remained vacant. It was not so easy to find a successor to Zinzendorf. A certain number of young and active brethren and sisters placed themselves at the disposal of the elders and were appointed as "assistants" in the various offices and services of the Church.

Chapter 16

A Multitude of Adversaries

Some time previously, the Count had thought it necessary to make a public declaration with respect to Herrnhut, to correct the chimerical accounts of it then current in the world. He had arranged that some of the Brethren should give an explanation of several essential points before a notary, and that the document should be signed by them and by the pastor, as well as by himself.

This precaution, singular as it may seem, was not superfluous for the new community had become the object of public curiosity and had given rise to suppositions the most malevolent and to judgments the most erroneous and severe. It was at Zinzendorf that they were chiefly aimed. By some he was regarded as a fanatic, by others he was accused of "indifferentism." The largeness of his views and the comprehensiveness of his tolerance gave rise to reproach. As a matter of fact, he *was* indifferent to many things to which the theologians of his time attached supreme importance.

He believed that all who loved the Savior formed a spiritual unity infinitely above the barriers which the traditions, the rites, and even the errors of the various Churches had raised between each other. In a letter written in 1729, he says:

> Although I am and wish to remain a member of the Evangelical Church, I do not limit Christ and His truth to any sect. Whosoever believes that he is saved by the grace of the Lord Jesus, by living faith, that is to say whosoever seeks and finds in Him wisdom, and righteousness, and sanctification, and redemption, he is my brother, and I regard it as a useless and even injurious task to examine into his opinions on other matters, and to sit in judgment on his exegesis. In this sense they are right who say that it does not much trouble me that some are heterodox, but only in this sense.

About the same time, also, Zinzendorf prepared a selection of sacred songs for the use of the Catholics of Germany, and he even took it into his head to seek for it the authorization of the Pope. He had no scruples in this matter, for he regarded the sovereign Pontiff as the legitimate head of those Christians who receive the Canons of the Council of Trent. "So long as the Pope adores Christ crucified," writes he, "and regards Him as his God, one cannot, according to the definition of St. John, consider him as anti-Christ."

Moreover, he revered the personal character of the man who then filled the Papal chair. Benedict XIII (Orsini), the last Pope furnished by the Dominican Order, was universally respected for his piety and rectitude as well as for his wisdom and tolerance. The project came to nothing. The letter asking for the Pope's approval of the volume was never sent. But the bare idea of writing to the Pope was quite enough to bring a nest of hornets round the poor Count's head; and there were not wanting those who more than hinted that the desire of his heart was a cardinal's hat!

If the large and tolerant spirit of Zinzendorf exposed him to the charge of apostasy, his horror of interference on the part of the police in religious matters furnished a pretext to others for a charge of anarchy. Zinzendorf an anarchist! It is quite true that his principles were in advance of his time. On many points they were in advance of ours. A pastor, one of his friends, complained to him, in a letter of the little support that he gave to authority; that he might have very effectually helped him in his ministry if he had prohibited various public diversions, etc. etc. Zinzendorf replied:

> No, it is impossible to put the yoke of Christ on men against their will, and until they have been converted. To exercise an external constraint, to forbid worldly diversions, is the way to make hypocrites, and to produce the most frightful secret abominations. It is the way to make men mock at all authority, and to embitter them against the ministers of reconciliation. It also is the way to make men satisfied with themselves, simply because they abstain from those diversions with which others sometimes amuse themselves.

After this, it is rather amusing to hear the Count accused of Pharisaism. Yet this was the chief reproach cast upon him by men of the world, nor by them alone. Many ministers represented Zinzendorf and the Brethren as the false prophets of the Gospels "who come to you in sheep's clothing, but inwardly they are ravening wolves." It gratified the ill-humor of the old orthodox school that had been disturbed out of its easy habits by the prodigious activity of the Count, who had overstepped the limits of their liturgies and outrun all their programs. These meetings, these institutions, these bands, these choirs, a young count making theology! All these things perplexed and disconcerted them. No sooner had Spener been silenced and the Church begun to enjoy a little repose, than up starts this new disturber of the peace, and everywhere you hear talk of nothing but the Revival!

But these attacks, violent as they were, were not so keenly felt by Zinzendorf as were those that came from his former friends, from those even with whom he had believed himself to be in perfect spiritual communion, and from whom he had hoped to receive support against the enmity of the theologians of the old school. We refer to the Pietists. "My own mother's children were angry with me!" he exclaims.

We have seen that Franke, though to the end of his life he remained on terms of friendship with Zinzendorf, did not altogether approve of his tendencies. But others—a certain pastor named Mischke, e.g., in whose behalf the Count had pleaded to save him from persecution—roundly declared that they considered him to be still unconverted, because, according to his own avowal, he had not gone through what they called the "struggle of repentance." These accusations troubled him for a moment, and drove him "closer to the Savior's bleeding side." After a careful review of the way the Lord had led him, he received an assurance so clear and deep and sweet that he was, in truth, not merely a servant but a son of God, that all his momentary doubts for ever fled away.

From that moment also he perceived that he was not in perfect harmony with the system of the Pietists, and he no longer hesitated to speak out against their absolute method and their too rigid rules. The following extract from his *Natural Reflections* gives his opinions on this subject, and furnishes a curious specimen of his style:

What they call *agon pœnitentiœ* (the struggle of repentance) can be nothing but a kind of spiritual convulsion, resulting either from the opposition produced in the patient between the action of the malady and the will that he has to be healed, or from resistance to the duties prescribed by the law. I do not in the least deny the existence of these two kinds of conflict. I admit that it is infinitely better that a child should have convulsions whilst cutting its teeth than that it should die during during the process; but I have never known a doctor so much a man of system as to forbid children to get their teeth without convulsions.

It would indeed be sad to see theologians pitiless at this point, and when a soul, without spiritual convulsions, is born of the Spirit, and placed in the arms of the Good Shepherd, insisting that it shall be thrown to the wolves because mother and child have not conducted themselves according to their rules.

I am well aware that the spiritual birth is not effected without suffering; but as to determining the degree of pain that one must feel, as to praising up this "struggle of repentance" practiced by these accoucheurs (midwives) of the soul, who bungle a thousand times for one happy deliverance, not even the Confession of Augsburg, even if it were to insist upon it, could persuade me to practice it. It is far better to keep to the teaching of the New Testament, and even to the Old. "Of His own will He begat us" (James 1:18). "The wind bloweth where it listeth: so is every one that is born of the Spirit" (John 3:8).

These declarations only served to strengthen the bad opinion that the Pietists had already of the Count. They accused him of a want of gravity, of a vivacity bordering on levity. The paradoxical tone that he loved to give to his language also scandalized them, and still more his frankness. For instance, "when any one spoke of a certain doctrine that was not yet dear to him, he avowed quite openly that he had no conviction on the subject. This, of course, did not mean that he denied the doctrine, but to them it came to the same thing."

The opposition of the pietists became more and more pronounced and more and more direct. Zinzendorf, on his side, became wearied of their spirit of legality, of their affected austerity, and especially of the moral constraint that they diffused around them. Never, however, did he return their attacks, and on one occasion only did he lose his patience.

We have passed in review many classes of the adversaries of Zinzendorf, but we are not yet at the end of them. "I wish you much success," the famous jurist, Thomasius, had said to him some years before, "for the name of those that will oppose you will be legion." The prediction was fulfilled.

The year 1729 showered pamphlets against him. He was known by very few, but he was condemned by almost all. Some one cried "Fire!" and then the crowd caught up the cry, although they did not know where the fire was, or whether there really was a fire at all. The servant was not above his Lord. The malice of his enemies did not even scruple to attempt to cast a shadow over the holiness of the Count's personal life. The attempt failed most signally. Then they made his very sanctity a ground of attack. They accused him of self-righteousness and said that he was trying to atone by legal works for his doctrinal and ecclesiastical heterodoxy.

But Zinzendorf did not reply to the contradictory accusations that poured in from all sides. He left his conduct to the judgment of Him that readeth the heart. On one occasion only at this period did he break his rule. After reading a pamphlet which, amongst other things, charged him with rejecting infant baptism, he sent the author a note informing him that the Countess had just presented him with a son, and inviting his accuser to do him the favor of standing as one of the sponsors.

Chapter 17

Pastoral Activity

After a short visit to Berleberg, in Westphalia, Zinzendorf returned to Herrnhut, and resumed his ministerial activities. We shall not follow him into all the details of this pastoral life, but select a few characteristic particulars.

His solicitude for those whom the Lord had committed to his care knew no bounds. If one of them, for example, wished to converse with him about the state of his soul, he was careful not to let slip what might be the only favorable moment. He made it a rule never to defer or to abridge by a moment a conversation of this kind, even if it kept him up the whole night. Often he might say, "The zeal of Thine house hath eaten me up."

He writes in his *Journal* for February 16, 1731: "Today I have been in continual anguish on account of certain affairs of the community. If such days are often repeated I shall die. But all this is seed for eternity. There is not one of our tears that is not treasured up."

He did not allow any fault to pass without a reprimand, especially among the workers of the Church. But this was not the reprimand of a superior making use of his authority. It was the warning of a brother repenting with his brothers, encouraging them, and praying with them. He did not estimate the various sins in the ordinary way.

For instance, when any one had fallen into the grosser sins of the flesh, Zinzendorf was so moved with grief that he often wept over the guilty person; and, if he saw him despairing because of his fault, he would console him, so filled was he with compassion for a man whom God had punished with the most terrible of punishments, he thought, by letting him fall into sin.

To other faults, on the contrary, which are ordinarily more easily pardoned, he was extremely severe. When he came across an instance of pride, for instance, or of envy or bitterness or spite, he was like a lion let loose. He would listen to no excuses, and he could not be appeased. He could not bear either that anyone should pretend to be different from what he really was. If a man declared that he felt no disposition to give his heart to the Savior, Zinzendorf would say that his time would come, and that in the meantime the man must be treated with the same regard and the same charity as those whom they reckoned among the faithful. But hypocrisy he abominated.

A woman, who had recently come to Herrnhut, was in the habit of talking a great deal about her spiritual misery, and about her desire to be saved. She said she had prayed, but the Lord was deaf to her cry. Some things about her cast a doubt on the truth of her words, but she always vehemently protested her sincerity. One day, the Count was speaking in a meeting on the sin of hypocrisy, and while he was dwelling on the case of Ananias and Sapphira the woman fell down unconscious, and when she recovered she confessed that up to that moment she had persisted in the most detestable deception.

Here is another example of a different kind, but one that will equally illustrate the power of the Spirit as manifested in the work of the Count. A man of the name of Münster, an old resident at Herrnhut, who had fallen from grace and lost all confidence in God, became so melancholy that he determined secretly to leave the place. The Count had long been concerned about his state, but had never felt called to speak to him directly. One evening, however, he had an impression that he ought to go at once and see him. He ran to his house. It was just ten o'clock, the hour that Münster had fixed for his flight. The Count met him coming out of his door, and asked him how he was. "Not well," he growled. The Count then spoke to him with so much sympathy and affection that the man burst into tears, abandoned his resolution, turned again to God, and to the end remained a faithful member of the Church.

The care of the sick was a marked feature in the church life of Herrnhut. Zinzendorf believed that the cure of the body must begin in the soul. He was persuaded that God had some special design in each particular ailment that He permitted, and that it is our business, first of all, to find out what that design is. Once we have discovered the final cause of the malady, and taken the warning or learnt the lesson it is meant to convey, we may ask and hope to be healed.

Many cases of sudden cure were witnessed in answer to prayer and faith. The Count rejoiced in them and thanked God for them from the bottom of his heart. He himself had received marvelous answers to prayer. Nevertheless he feared lest the Brethren should make too much of these things, and therefore he spoke of them as quite simple and ordinary occurrences. He reminded them that miracles were not for believers, but for unbelievers, and that the gift of working miracles, even if they should obtain the gift, is no proof that the miracle worker is a child of God. And, finally, he told them that they should not seek after such gifts, because the essential thing is to love Christ and commit themselves to Him.

Chapter 18

Foundation of Moravian Missions

Perceiving that the Saxon Government was not too favorable to Herrnhut, Zinzendorf deemed that it might be prudent to transfer his allegiance to the King of Denmark, and place the new community under his patronage and protection. He thought, moreover, that in the service of the Danish king he would be able to exchange the civil for the ecclesiastical state without exciting so much observation and remark. He, therefore, started for Copenhagen in April 1731, accompanied by a few of the Brethren.

They were well received at the Danish Court, but the project came to nothing, and the Count returned home more disgusted than ever with the pomps and vanities of the world. He had learnt that a pious court is none the less a court, and, as he said to the Countess:

> If there is a work to be done at court, I am not the man to do it. I could not spend my time over such trifles as make up the daily life of courtiers and of kings. I dare not appear before God with the responsibility incurred by frittering away my days in such puerilities.

The visit to Copenhagen was not so fruitless, however, as the Count believed. It was the starting point of the Missions of the Brethren. It will be remembered that the desire to send the Gospel to the heathen was one of the earliest desires of his heart. Well, during his stay in Copenhagen, the Count had come across two Greenlanders who had made him acquainted with the work of Father Egedius, a Roman Catholic missionary in their country. The work of this faithful missionary had been almost fruitless, and Zinzendorf was greatly distressed to hear that the mission was regarded as hopeless.

At the same time, the Count had met with a converted negro from the West Indies belonging to Count Laurwig. He talked with him about the condition of his unconverted brethren. The poor man drew a lamentable picture of the oppression and corruption of the negroes, and assured the Count that many of them would welcome the preaching of the Gospel. "And," added he, with touching simplicity, "I have a sister who I am sure would be converted if she only heard of Jesus."

Zinzendorf was greatly moved. He saw at a glance the work to which the Lord was calling him. The thought never left him. In a transport of hope he wrote to the Countess:

> Yesterday Count Laurwig talked very amicably with me. He would like to come and see us. He has given me permission to bring his colored servant Anthony to see Herrnhut, and to open up the way for the conversion of the negroes of Africa and America. The Danish missions to Greenland and Lapland have been abandoned. The ground is clear. I see a vast field opening up before me. May God vouchsafe to say "Amen"!

On his return to Hermhut (in July 1731) the Count spoke of what he had seen and heard in Copenhagen. His words produced such an effect on Leonard Dober that, on the spot, he resolved, if the Lord would, he would offer himself for work among the blacks. Tobias Leupold formed the same resolution. They prayed together and made known their desire to the Lord. They afterwards wrote to Zinzendorf without mentioning their names.

When the negro arrived from Copenhagen, he was requested to speak in an assembly. He set forth the deplorable condition of the negro slaves, but stated that it would be impossible for any one to get access to them without himself becoming a slave and working with them in the plantation. Dober and Leupold were not dismayed. Their resolution was confirmed. The matter was considered in the Council of the Community, and it was decided, after a period of preparation, to send the Brethren out. This was the beginning of the Moravian Missions to the West Indies—missions greatly blessed. Two other Brethren volunteered at the same time for Greenland, and, after a period of waiting and testing, they also were sent forth. Spangenberg comments:

> I must admit that, at this time, neither the Count nor the Brethren knew how to win the heart of the heathen. All they knew was that this work of missions was a big affair. They also knew that this, pre-eminently, was one of those matters on which it was necessary to be "of one accord" in order to "remind the Lord" effectually. But, as they had no experience to guide them, the Count preferred to give these first missionaries no instructions, but simply to "commend them to God and to the word of His grace."

As we shall presently see, the later missionaries were sent out in a more formal way. Nevertheless, when once they were upon their stations, they were allowed to act with a very free hand, and to adapt themselves to the circumstances and the needs of the various mission fields.

Chapter 19

First Exile; Visits Tübingen

Largely through the indiscretion of his relatives in harboring refugees who were obnoxious to the Government, Zinzendorf was exiled from his estates in the early part of 1733. He had resolved to visit Tübingen in order to acquaint the Theological Faculty with the doctrines and the polity of Herrnhut and to submit to it the following question: "Can the Unity of the Brethren, whilst retaining its own discipline, remain united to the Evangelical Church?" It will be easily understood how important a matter this was to the Brethren. They were continually being reproached with their want of conformity to Lutheran teaching; and it would be an immense advantage to them if they could secure the *imprimatur* of a university so famous and so influential as Tübingen.

Soon after his arrival, Zinzendorf had a serious illness, but during his recovery, he had an opportunity to carry out his mission, many of the professors waiting upon him and receiving his statements with interest and cordiality. Being asked what he meant by Christian union, about which he talked so much, he replied: "It is hard to say, but it is easy to do;" and, when he saw the astonishment created by his answer, he added: "Christians have only to devote to the cause of Jesus as much zeal and energy as men of the world devote to business, and the communion of saints will soon be realized."

As soon as he was well enough, he made an evangelistic tour in the vicinity of Tübingen and Stuttgart. Everywhere he was heartily received, and his message was blessed to many souls. The most distinguished men of Wurtemberg, among whom we may name the illustrious commentator Bengel, showed him many marks of affection and esteem. This greatly humbled him. "In Lusatia," he wrote to the Countess, "I have to bear opprobrium, but I am much more troubled by the high esteem in which they hold me here. This is a cross to me indeed."

All this time, the Tübingen divines were considering the question proposed to them. Their answer was unanimously in the affirmative. They were quite aware that their decision might cause offence to some, but they said to Zinzendorf: "It is worth some risk to promote the cause of God." The Faculty gave their decision in due form on the 19th of April. "Thus," says Schrautenbach, "the constitution of the new Church ratified at Herrnhut by the judgment of God on the 7th of January 1731, was confirmed at Tübingen by the judgment of men on the 19th of April, 1733."

Zinzendorf left Tübingen delighted with his success, and returned to Ebersdorf. He learnt that the new Elector of Saxony was much more favorable to Herrnhut than his predecessor, who had died during the absence of the Count. One of his first acts was to grant the freedom of his States to the Moravian emigrants. The Count himself received permission to return.

To this general act of toleration, there was, however, one exception. The disciples of Schwenkfeld were exempted, and were expressly ordered to quit the country. We mention this apparently trifling and extraneous matter because of what sprang from it. It would hardly be too much to say that the Methodist Church sprang from it. No circumstance in modern history was more clearly providential; for it was a party of these Moravian exiles whose calmness, and devotion, and brotherly love so deeply impressed John Wesley during their voyage across the Atlantic, on their way to Georgia, and led the great founder of Methodism to form the acquaintance of Peter Böhler, who brought him into the joy and strength of experimental religion.

Chapter 20

The Count Seeks Ordination

Zinzendorf had not abandoned his resolve to enter the ministry, but the circumstances detailed in the last few chapters had prevented him from carrying it out. He made up his mind to put the matter off no longer. In vain did the Countess seek to dissuade him.

"God calls me to preach the Gospel," said he, "and it is not the same whether I bear my witness in an ordinary meeting or in a church and from a pulpit. I want to preach my crucified Redeemer to men of all sorts, and I want to do it in conformity with the established order and without seeming to wish to be singular."

Before he had time to think how his resolution could be carried out, an unexpected way was opened up. A pious merchant at Stralsund, of the name of Richter, who was quite unknown to him, wrote to Zinzendorf asking him if he could recommend a tutor for his sons. Zinzendorf at once determined to accept the post for himself. He saw an opportunity to reside for a while *incognito* in Stralsund, and pass an examination in the presence of the two distinguished theologians of that town—Langemak and Sibeth. He therefore replied that the tutor Richter asked for would come.

On the 29th of March, 1734, he presented himself to Richter as the expected tutor, under the name of Louis de Freydeck (one of the titles of the Count) and began at once to teach the boys. Soon afterwards he presented himself to Langemak, who took him for a candidate for the ministry, and gave him a preaching appointment. He later reflected:

> We talked together about all sorts of things, and in the course of conversation he showed me the sketch of a pamphlet he was writing to refute Count Zinzendorf and the Herrnhuters. I asked him, quite simply, if he had read their writings, and, on his answering that he

had not. I got him to promise that he would—with what result is now well known.

After preaching a trial sermon, Zinzendorf made himself known to the two theologians, who afterwards examined him for three whole days, in Latin and in German, on every point of Christian doctrine. Other trial sermons followed, under one of which the venerable Langemak was moved to tears, and so deeply was his conscience quickened that he who came as judge went away a penitent.

At last, on the 26th of April, the two doctors delivered a detailed report of the examination to the Count, together with a certificate of orthodoxy, and he returned to Herrnhut, after placing his sword of State into the hands of Langemak.

It now only remained to seek some competent authority to induct him formally into the office of the ministry. He applied to the Theological Faculty of Tubingen:

> I wish to follow the example of Stephanas, with whom St. Paul was so much pleased, and addict myself to the ministry of the saints (1 Cor. 16:15). I wish to win souls to my beloved Savior, to make them His friends, to gather His flock, to hire laborers for Him. I shall continue, if the Lord will, to devote myself first of all to the community whose servant I have been since 1727, and, under its auspices, I shall also address myself to distant peoples that know nothing of the merits of the blood of Jesus and of the salvation which is found through it.

The Faculty at once acceded to the Count's request, and granted him the authority desired. A short time afterwards he was formally ordained.

Chapter 21

His Theological and Spiritual Development

The external events in the life of the Count must not preclude from our consideration the still more important development of his intellectual and spiritual life. The reproaches continually cast upon him by his enemies, and the arguments by which Dippel of Berlebourg, whom he had encountered some years before, continued to attack the doctrine of Redemption, led him to examine afresh the foundations of his faith. He wished to study the teachings of Scripture as profoundly as possible. He therefore sought the assistance of Rothe and Spangenberg (a young theologian whom he had met at Jena, and who afterwards, became Zinzendorf's assistant and successor) and two other divines, who were then at Herrnhut, and began with them a series of "Biblical Conferences."

This new study of the Bible, accompanied as it was by a careful examination of his own heart, led him to see more clearly than ever that the expiatory sacrifice of Christ is the very center of Christianity, and that all true piety must be founded in living faith in the crucified Redeemer, and in fellowship with Him—a fellowship which springs from that faith. Speaking of this period, Zinzendorf says:

> Dippel's system appeared to aim at the suppression of the idea of wrath in God, and, so long as I regarded it from that angle it did not shock me, for I was at that time much occupied with theodicy,[4] and it troubled me not to be able to give to His acts a sufficiently mathematical consistency. I sought at all costs to justify Him in the eyes of reasonable men; so that the assertions of Dippel did not alarm me.
>
> But when I came to account to myself for my conversion, I perceived that there was, in the necessity for the death of Jesus, and

4. An explaination why a perfectly good, almighty, all-knowing God permits evil.

> in that word ransom, a very profound mystery, a mystery before which philosophy stands still, confounded, but to which revelation clings with the utmost tenacity. This gave me a new insight into the whole doctrine of salvation. I made the experiment first on my own heart, then on Dippel (but he was carried away by the ardor of his polemic), and finally on my Brethren and companions in toil. And since the year 1734, the expiatory sacrifice of Jesus has been and will for ever remain, our treasure, our device, our all: our panacea for all evil, whether in doctrine or practice.

Henceforth, salvation through the atoning sacrifice of Jesus became the sole theology of the Brethren. The Biblical phrases "the Lamb slain," the "stripes by which we are healed," "the blood which cleanses from all sin," were those which they preferred to use. They are found on every page of their writings, and in all their hymns, and constitute, if we may so express it, "the local color" of Herrnhut. It is this that Zinzendorf, in his energetic language, calls "the theology of blood," just as he usually calls his church, "the Church of the Lamb." "The blood of Christ," says he, "is, in the kingdom of Christ, what money is in the world, nervus *rerum agendarum* (the driving force)."

No doubt a too exclusive preoccupation with this side of the work of salvation has hindered the development of Christian speculation among the Moravian Brethren, and stamped a sort of uniformity upon their preaching of the Gospel; but it is also certain that this immovable attachment to the central and capital fact of Christianity has been their strength, and has saved them from many errors. While some other Protestant communions have had to stop and lay again the foundations of the doctrine of Christ, the little Church of the Brethren has left these things behind, and by its schools, its ministers and its missionaries, has labored to spread the Gospel and to build the holy temple on the one foundation once for ever laid.

Chapter 22

Home Missionary Tours; Conversion of Crellius

While the Brethren were occupied in sending the Gospel to the heathen, Zinzendorf employed himself in home missionary work. A tour which he made in Switzerland in the autumn of 1735 was greatly blessed. He walked most of the way from Zurich to Constance, and, contrary to his custom, he made the journey alone. He looked upon the tour as a kind of retreat in which he might be able to converse continually with his invisible Friend, to Whom he liked to talk as he walked as if He had been walking by his side.

Traveling of this kind could not have been easy for the Count. He used to walk with his head erect and seldom looked to the ground. He was, moreover, near-sighted and always absorbed in his thoughts. He often stumbled and sometimes lost his way. What was worse still, he had little regard for money, and hardly knew the value of the different coins in use. His purse was often empty; for, when he met a beggar on the road, he regarded it as a God-sent opportunity for doing good. From this cause, he was sometimes brought into straits himself.

One day, for instance, he went into a house, exhausted with fatigue, and asked for some food, exhibiting at the same time the money that remained in his purse. It was only a few farthings. The people smiled, and sent him away fasting. On another occasion, a more confiding peasant lent him a little money to enable him to complete his journey by coach.

Another tour, at this time, was still more fruitful and interesting. In March, 1736, he found himself in Amsterdam, where his sermons and his conversations were well received and followed by many signs of grace. Here, as elsewhere, he was specially attracted to men who were under the ban of persecution.

Amongst the Socinians of that city, he met with a famous divine called Samuel Crellius, known also by the name of Artemonius:

> On the morning of the 8th of March, the aged Crellius called upon me. The Lord opened my heart towards him, and we were very soon in the midst of a conversation. I told him quite plainly where I thought he was in error, declaring that the foundation of my faith was our great Savior, the living and eternal God. And he expounded to me his own belief. From that moment, he had so much confidence in me that he attended all our meetings while I remained in Amsterdam.
>
> He asked me one day if I believed that a man would be damned because he did not believe in the divinity of Jesus Christ. "All blasphemy against the Son of man shall be forgiven," said I; "but it is none the less a blasphemy and should not be persisted in."

This modest, sympathetic treatment was not lost upon the old Socinian.[5] After Zinzendorf left Amsterdam, Crellius kept up a correspondence with him, and soon transferred to the Savior the confidence with which the Count had inspired him. His two daughters entered the Church of the Brethren. The grace of Jesus followed him to the end of his days. A little before he died, he sent a farewell message of gratitude and love to the Moravian community. Then he called on "the Lamb of God," and expired while repeating the words of a hymn by Zinzendorf, which may be rendered by Charles Wesley's well-known lines:

I the chief of sinners am,
But Jesus died for me.

---

5. Someone who professes belief in God and the Scriptures but denies Christ's divinity.

Chapter 23

The Moravians and the Wesleys

For some inscrutable reason, but not, as will be evident, without Divine purpose, the Count was again banished from his estates. This second exile, to be followed by a much longer one, forms an epoch in the life of Zinzendorf. Henceforth, Herrnhut, though he returned to it to end his days, ceased to be the center of his activities. As we have seen, the need of diffusing the knowledge of his Savior pressed him more and more. He therefore submitted without much reluctance to the rigorous orders of the King. He saw in them a distinct call from the Lord, and an answer to reiterated prayers, and set out at once on that missionary career in which the larger part of his remaining life was spent.

We shall not follow him in all the details of his itinerancy in Europe and America, preaching the Gospel, holding conferences, confirming the churches, correcting abuses; nor shall we be able to more than glance at some of the more salient and important points in the subsequent development of his personal character and opinions. We shall confine ourselves to a few typical facts and events that may serve to complete the life, and prepare the way for the final estimate of the character of the Count.

By far the most important journey undertaken at this time was his visit to England in the early part of 1737. His primary object was to make the Church of the Brethren known to the authorities in the Church of England, and to open up the British Colonies to the Moravian missionaries. His first step was to put himself in communication with the Society for the Instruction of the Negroes in the British Plantations. This society, which was willing enough to avail itself of the zeal of the Brethren, resolved, in concert with the

Count, to seek the approbation of the Archbishop of Canterbury. His grace at once accorded it, declaring that he had long been acquainted with the Moravian Church; that it was an apostolic and Episcopal Church; that it did not profess any doctrine in opposition to the Thirty-nine Articles; and that recent conversations he had had with Count Zinzendorf had fully confirmed him in the opinion he had of it.

The Count did not preach publicly in England, but, as usual, his family worship was much frequented by pious persons who subsequently formed themselves into a little society. This was a very small affair, but the Count did not "despise the day of small things." The grain of mustard-seed was here as elsewhere to become a great tree.

The same blessing that rested on the Brethren in Germany accompanied their work in England. At the present moment (1890's), it is in the British Isles and in their American Colonies (now the United States), that two-thirds of the members and three-fourths of the communicants of the Moravian Church are found. Not by their direct action on the English religious revival of the eighteenth century only, but also by their influence on those who were to become the principal instruments in that revival, did the Moravians achieve distinction in the ecclesiastical history of the time. We refer, of course, to Whitefield and to the Wesleys. The *role* of these men is too important in the history of the Church to hurry over their relations with Zinzendorf, and with the Brethren in general.

About fifteen months before the arrival of the Count in England, John and Charles Wesley had gone to Georgia to convert the Indians "without being converted themselves." During the voyage out, as before observed, they were greatly struck by the humility, the charity, and the peace and joy amid the perils of the deep, of the Moravian passengers on board. Speaking of the terrific tempest they encountered, John Wesley says:

> At seven, I went to the Germans.... There was now an opportunity of trying whether they were delivered from the spirit of fear, as well as from that of pride, anger, and revenge.
>
> In the midst of the psalm wherewith their service began, the sea broke over, split the main sail in pieces, covered the ship,

> and poured in between the decks, as if the great deep had already swallowed it up. A terrible screaming began among the English. The Germans calmly sang on. I asked one of them afterwards, "Were you not afraid?" He answered, "I thank God, no." "But were not your women and children afraid?" He answered mildly, "No, our women and children are not afraid to die."

In Georgia, John Wesley met with Spangenberg, and Charles, returning to Europe before John, often met with Zinzendorf in London. The faith of these two men deeply impressed the two Wesleys, and their conversation made them feel what they needed in order to effectively preach the Gospel. However, the Lord, who did not employ either Peter or John to lay their hands on Paul, but a much humbler instrument—Ananias—had reserved to another the privilege of removing the scales from the eyes of the Wesleys.

At the end of 1737, a young Moravian minister, Peter Böhler, was about to start for Georgia. Before setting sail, however, he spent three months in London in the early part of 1738, and there he reaped a part of the harvest that Zinzendorf had sown. He soon saw what was wanting in the Wesleys, and set himself to bring them out of the twilight of their mystic and ascetic theology. "My brother, my brother," said he to one of them, "thou must purge thyself of thy philosophy."

Böhler answered all the difficulties raised by them, with a simple reference to the testimony of Scripture and recent examples of the omnipotence of grace. Under Böhler's teaching and testimony they came clearly to understand the doctrine of their own Church with respect to justification by faith.

But it was not under Böhler's ministry that they found peace with God and obtained the assurance of sonship and salvation. The account of John Wesley's "conversion," familiar as it is, is too important and too beautiful to be omitted here. Wednesday, May 24th, 1738, is a day never to be forgotten. To quote the words of the great founder of Methodism, who at the time was seeking God with all his heart:

> In the evening, I went very unwillingly to a society in Aldersgate Street, where one was reading Luther's *Preface to the Epistle to the Romans*. About a quarter to nine, while he was

> describing the change which God works in the heart through faith in Christ, I felt my heart strangely warmed. I felt I did trust in Christ, Christ alone, for salvation; and an assurance was given me that He had taken away *my* sins, even mine, and saved *me* from the law of sin and death.

A few weeks later, Wesley started for Germany. Before entering on that course of evangelism to which he felt himself so powerfully urged, he wished to acquaint himself more fully with those who had preceded him and pointed out the way. However high his hopes, Herrnhut surpassed them. In his *Journal,* he has left us a detailed account of his journey, and a full description of that "happy sojourn with a people among whom he would fain have spent his life, had not the Master called him to labor in another part of His vineyard."

"The spirit which reigns among the Brethren," wrote Charles Wesley, "is beyond our expectations. Young and old breathe nothing but faith and love, always and everywhere."

For some time the followers of Wesley and the followers of Zinzendorf held their meetings together but eventually divergences appeared. Wesley was the first to notice a tendency among the Moravians, as he thought, towards antinomianism and quietism. Zinzendorf, on the other hand, could not accept what he took to be Wesley's doctrine of "sinless perfection." Wesley's adherents, therefore, left the common meeting-house in Fetter lane, and took one of their own. From that time the two societies were separate organizations, and each, in its own way, did the work confided to it.

A now famous conversation between these two remarkable men took place in Gray's Inn Walks, London, on the 3rd of September, 1741, three years after Wesley's visit to Germany. It was carried on in Latin, in which language, doubtless, they found they could be mutually more intelligent than if Zinzendorf spoke broken English or Wesley imperfect German. The dialogue is given by the latter in his *Journal* in the original Latin, and a translation of it is furnished by Moore in his *Life of Wesley.* It referred exclusively to the doctrinal points on which they differed, and to the recent dissensions between the Methodists and Moravians in London. The interview was brought about by James Hutton, an early friend of the Wesleys, who by degrees became a Moravian.

We cannot pretend very much to regret this division between these holy and distinguished men. We are constrained, the rather, to admire the wisdom of God Who loves to diversify His operations, and Who, in this case, as in that of Paul and Barnabas, permitted the separation of His servants, in order that the Gospel seed might be more quickly and more widely sown.

Men dream of external unity and often pursue it at the expense of real unity, unity in truth and love, but God baffles their efforts. He stops the building of their Babels, and urges them towards freedom and diversity. It is vain for men to persist in seeing in diversity nothing but the principle of war. Both in His Church and in the natural world, God makes of it the principle of love and the source of life.

Though following different paths, the disciples of Wesley have cherished a fraternal, or rather a filial, affection for the Moravians. The Rev. Thomas Jackson in his *Life of Charles Wesley* (Vol. 1, page 282), says:

> The Wesleyan Society has incurred a debt of respect and gratitude towards the Moravian Brethren that it can never repay. John and Charles Wesley, however excellent their qualities, had found neither holiness nor happiness before they learnt from Peter Böhler that faith in Christ saves us from sin, from its guilt and from its dominion, that this faith is a gift of the Holy Spirit, acting on a penitent heart, and that it is followed immediately by the inward witness of the mercy of God and of our adoption. It is without doubt to this doctrine that Methodist preaching owes its efficacy and its success. No doubt God might have employed other means to convey it to the Wesleys, but He did not do so. Peter Böhler was the instrument through whom He was pleased to convey this benefit to them and through them to millions of souls.

On his side, Zinzendorf, who had criticized the Wesleys, spontaneously asked their pardon in a note that he added to one of his works that he published in English, in 1754. He recognized that, as they were not members of the Moravian Church, he had no right to judge them. He declared that he had been wrong in doing so, and promised for the future not to commit the same fault.

Chapter 24

Visit to the West Indies and America

Early in 1739, Zinzendorf paid a visit to the West Indies. At the beginning of the voyage we meet with an interesting example of his familiar intercourse with the Savior. He was very subject to sea-sickness, but on this occasion he had a peculiar dread of it, for he had marked out for himself a large amount of work that he wished to finish on the voyage: "As I had a great deal to do, I said to the Savior that it would be very inconvenient for me to be sick for long, and assuredly He cured me before we had well set sail."

The voyage was not without its dangers, but they reached the Island of St. Thomas in safety on the 29th of January, 1739. The Moravian Mission there was in the most deplorable state. The missionaries had been well received by the Negroes, who had flocked to hear the Gospel from their lips and upwards of nine hundred of them had been saved. But this revival of religion had greatly incensed the planters. They added to the burdens and oppressions of the Negroes, and did all they could to stop the preachers' mouths.

Some of them complained to the Governor that the missionaries wished to teach the Negroes to be better Christians than their masters; they accused them of administering baptism without authority, which was not true; what was more true was that the missionaries objected to taking an oath. They had therefore been arrested and cast into prison, and might have perished from sickness and misery but for the timely interposition of Zinzendorf. The Governor, thinking that the Count had great influence at Court, readily responded to his appeal, and not only released the missionaries, but gave permission to the Count to labor among the Negroes. This he did with great success. The persecutions endured by the Brethren had made a great impression on the colored population, and when the Count began to preach, they flocked around him, eager to receive from his lips the consolations and the promises of the Gospel.

If the arrival of Zinzendorf was opportune, his departure from St. Thomas was not less timely, for at the moment of his embarkation, a messenger had been dispatched from Copenhagen with orders to the Governor to arrest him and put him in prison. Zinzendorf was back again in Europe when the messenger arrived.

This brief journey to the West Indies seems to have impaired the health of Zinzendorf, and, in the end of the year 1740, he quite broke down beneath the burden of his duties and his cares. For some time his soul, like the Psalmist's, was "cast down within him," and he was ready to despair. To heal him of this despondency, God seems to have dealt with him homeopathically: a method of treatment which seeks to irritate the evil so as to bring it the sooner to an end. One trouble followed hard upon another, until, in desperation, he set out once more to cross the Atlantic, this time for the United States. He abandoned his family, his friends, his still unfinished work in Europe, in order to expose himself to the perils of the deep and to the attacks of pirates, with no defense but God. This act of absolute reliance on his invisible Master seems to have perfectly restored his courage and his faith. In the extremity of his weakness he had found that strength was perfected, and thenceforth he was enabled both to triumph and to glory in the Lord.

We need not dwell upon the years that Zinzendorf devoted to the Christian Churches in America, nor have we space to touch upon his interviews with various Indian tribes. To illustrate the way in which his faith was perfected, we desire to quote in detail the remarkable account that has been handed down of one of those deliverances by which his path was strewn.

During the return voyage, on February 14th, 1743, the vessel neared the rocks of Scilly, and, a violent wind arising, they were in the utmost danger of being dashed to pieces. The passengers and crew were terrified, but Zinzendorf, who had preserved the greatest calmness, came forth from communion with his Savior and declared that they would reach the land in perfect safety. The ship's captain relates the following:

He was in such high spirits that I was astounded. Seeing that I was still alarmed, he declared that in two hours the tempest would be over. I hardly took any notice of him, so unlikely did this seem, and, as usual in such circumstances, I began to pray and to prepare myself for death. When the two hours had passed, he fetched me on the quarter deck to look at the weather. We had not been there many minutes before the storm abated, the wind veered to the south-west, and we were out of danger.

I was dumfounded. We then went down to the main deck, and the Count summoned all on board to join him in thanking God for this merciful and marvelous deliverance. I was curious to know how he had been able so exactly to predict the moment when the storm would cease. I therefore asked him, and here is his reply: "I will tell you frankly," said he, "for I am sure you will not abuse my confidence. For twenty years, now, I have lived in intimate intercourse with my Savior. Now, when I find myself in peril, the first thing I do is carefully to inquire whether it is my fault that I am in these circumstances. If it is, I cast myself at the Savior's feet and ask Him to forgive me. This He always does, and often He reveals to me the issue of the affair. If He does not deign to reveal it, I keep calm, for I am sure that it is better for me not to know. But, in this instance, He was pleased to let me know that the storm would last for two hours longer."

This was very strange to me, for all my life I had heard much more about the greatness and the wrath of God than about His love for us poor creatures. But I believed what Zinzendorf said, for all through the voyage every thing that he said and did fully convinced me that he was a true and faithful servant of Jesus Christ.

It was during this voyage that Zinzendorf composed the hymn:

> Jesu, Thy blood and righteousness
> My beauty are, my glorious dress.

Chapter 25

Embarrassments and Aberrations

On his return from America, and for many years afterwards, the Count was besieged by difficulties from many quarters and of many kinds.

Again and again, as the community increased and as their missions extended, Zinzendorf was brought into financial straits by his lavish generosity, and by his anxiety to save the Brethren from bankruptcy. At his death, it was found that he had left a debt of 1,631,766 thalers, or £350,000. (Probably at that time the British pound would have been equivalent to $5.00 or even more so that the amount would have been at least $1,750,000). This debt, which exceeded the value of his estates and goods, was contracted wholly in the interests of the community. It was assumed by them, and was honorably and entirely extinguished in the course of fifty years. During the Count's lifetime, however, these monetary troubles sometimes weighed upon his mind.

But what harassed and embarrassed him still more was the persistent persecution and criticism to which he was exposed. We need not dwell again upon the action of the civil powers towards one whose utterly unworldly conduct had perplexed and scandalized them. Nor, with one exception, shall we mention the innumerable onslaughts on the Count and the community by the ordinary theologians of the time. The exception to which we allude was the opposition of a man who was not an ordinary theologian, and who had always been regarded by the Count with great affection and esteem.

Bengel had hitherto regarded Zinzendorf with sympathy and done full justice to his piety, but now began to consider the doings at Herrnhut as "a disquieting phenomenon." He contested the right of the Herrnhuters to be considered the successors of the ancient Church of the Brethren. He reproached them with founding their theology on feeling rather than knowledge. And, lastly, he maintained that the time had not yet come, as Zinzendorf pretended, to gather together the children of God. This last objection rested on the particular views Bengel was then expounding in his *Commentary on the Apocalypse.*

The most serious of Bengel's reproaches is the second, and it must be admitted that, at this period, Zinzendorf and his followers laid themselves open to the criticisms of both friends and foes. Not only feeling but imagination also colored their theology, and a growing contempt of public opinion led them into many eccentricities and extravagances both of speech and action.

"At that time," writes the candid Spangenberg, "Zinzendorf formed the habit of isolating himself much more than formerly, for purposes of communion and recuperation. But the habit grew upon him to such an extent that he became almost a hermit in the midst of the community, and this was good for neither him nor them."

The fact is that Zinzendorf was much too imaginative for solitude. We have often admired the way in which this faculty was tempered and balanced by his rare good sense and his submission to the Word of God. But sense, like every other faculty, needs to be maintained and cultivated. Social life is its vital air, solitude is its bane. The man who lives alone becomes indulgent to his own, and wanders from the common sense. His favorite ideas become fixed ideas, and his opinions principles. It was in this way that Zinzendorf, departing from the rule he had laid down that he would hold to the simplicity of Scripture, came to attach undue importance to certain speculative views. At the Synod of Marienborn in 1743, for example, he proposed that they should consider whether there is not ground to believe that the Holy Spirit is the mother of the faithful, just as God the Father is their father in Christ, and as Christ is the husband of the Church.

"We know by experience," said he, "as well as by Scripture, that the Holy Spirit teaches us, warns us, chastises us, guides us, brings us up for Christ. In short, that He does for us what a mother does for her children."

It is true that afterwards he regretted these speculations, and publicly repudiated them, ordering that all reference to them should be expunged from his writings, and thanking God that He had "saved him from the fire with which he had played before he was consumed."

"It is for us an unspeakable blessing," he said in the last year of his life, "that we have begun to understand this: that to penetrate into the mystery of the Trinity, or into any other transcendent verity and to draw from it definite conceptions, is to pluck the fruit of the forbidden tree."

Nevertheless, it is easy to see that not unfriendly theologians, at this time, had some ground for their aversion and distrust. His paradoxical way of speaking also gave a handle to his enemies. "He merely wished," says Spangenberg, "to arrest attention and to make men think. He therefore made use of many uncommon expressions, and introduced a language unknown to theologians. This would perhaps have done but little harm, if his adversaries had taken the trouble to inquire what he meant by these unusual terms. As it was, this habit led to many misunderstandings and disputes."

These and other peculiarities had a most mischievous effect on his followers. The disciples exaggerated the master. The copy, as is too oft the case, caricatured the original. At first, they employed paradoxes to give greater distinctness to the truth. By-and-by they used them for the sake of using them. The consequences were most serious. By way of felicitating themselves on being nothing but "poor sinners," they came to speak with some disdain of "sanctification." Zinzendorf had commended childlike simplicity as one of the most beautiful traits in the Christian character. They ended by becoming childish.

His very language formed a school. They wished to equal him in originality, and surpassed him in oddity and whimsicality. From all this, there resulted a poetico-theological jargon, intelligible to none but the initiated—a most mischievous quietism, a false liberty, an affected joy, much wanting in seriousness and dignity. In a word, a foolish and ludicrous Pietism, much more opposed to the sacred serenity of the Christian than the moroseness of the school of Spener.

This pitiful tendency predominated among the Brethren for five years—from 1744 or 1745 to 1750. But the Lord was faithful. The fascination ceased and the community came through the crisis humbler and more influential than before. Satan had desired to sift them as wheat, but Jesus had prayed for them, and their faith had not entirely failed. It is in this way that the Moravians speak of this phase of their development. They call it the *Zeit der Sichtung,* the sifting time.

Zinzendorf himself, the involuntary cause of these aberrations, was carried away by the current. Without thinking what he was doing he imitated his imitators, and followed his imagination into most adventurous and dangerous ways, as many of his verses show. Not even his enemies accused him or his followers of immorality; nor were they guilty of anything worse than childishness and impropriety, and of a certain lusciousness and too great familiarity of language in addressing their Redeemer. But their conduct, as the Count was ready to admit, had given legitimate occasion of offence to thoughtful, sober-minded men. On emerging from this period, we find him writing thus:

> The trial through which we have passed has been short but terrible. I was, myself, probably the cause of it, by expressing an idea that I have never been able and am not now able to abandon, viz., that, in order to enjoy all the benefits purchased and acquired for us by the death of Jesus, it is necessary for us to become little children to the very bottom of our hearts. I was penetrated by this idea, and on my return from America, I sought to instill it into my brethren. They received the idea and were quite carried away by it. But that which was at the first only a small group of persons, truly children, had soon become a large society, and in a few years has considerably degenerated. The abuse sprang from the fact that they were willing to have the joyfulness, but not the simplicity, the sincerity, the rectitude of childhood.

Chapter 26

Last Days and Death

There is something peculiarly solemn in the departure from the world of an apostle of the Lord, and one can hardly fail to pause in silence at one's entrance on the story of the closing days. The death of Zinzendorf was in keeping with his life. He was one of those blessed servants whom the Master finds watching when He calls them to Himself, with girded loins, and lighted lamp, and ready feet. The desire to depart and be with Christ had become habitual with him. Only the familiar intercourse that he enjoyed with his Savior and the delight he had in His service moderated that desire. During the months immediately preceding it, he did not express to his friends any presentiment of the end, but they might have gathered from the Count's redoubled energy and multiplied activities that he felt the end was near. In the beginning of the year 1760, he set himself to converse personally with every member, young and old, of the now numerous Church at Herrnhut, and four months after, when he died, it was found that he had almost carried out his purpose. It was also in his mind to spend the spring at Zeitz, but the health of his second wife (Anna Nitschmann, whom, on the advice of the Church, he had married after the death of the Countess in 1756) prevented him, and soon after he fell ill himself.

On the 5th of May, although he had slept badly, he rose early, and insisted on finishing before noon the task he had set himself for that day. On a brother urging him to finish the work another day, he answered gaily, "No; it is only good to rest after one's work is done." He therefore continued to write; and when he had finished what he had in hand he said, "There, now I may rest." He dined at table for the last time, but ate little, and complained of a burning thirst. After dinner he composed a hymn of over thirty verses for a meeting in the evening. At night he attended a love-feast, but retired soon after, much fatigued. All next day he kept his bed, and the catarrhal fever from which he was suffering increased in violence. His mind was clear and active, but a stubborn cough prevented him from speaking much. He was able, however, to tell his friends that his soul was kept in perfect peace, and to express the pleasure that he felt at the arrival of his old friend Frederick Watteville, and his nephew, Count de Reuss.

During the next night, the "workers" of the Church took their turns in watching by his bed. He recognized them with affection, but could not talk much with them. He grew weaker and weaker, but on the 8th he seemed a little more composed, and lavished on his relatives a wealth of tenderness and love. To them and to some others, he exclaimed:

> I cannot tell you how I love you. I am almost at Home now. And, indeed, are we not all of one mind like the angels, and as if we were in heaven? Who would have believed that the prayer of Jesus, "that they may be one," could be so beautifully answered here on earth?

While he was speaking, his face shone with joy and love. He afterwards talked about many of the brethren and sisters who had entered into the joy of their Lord. During the afternoon he finished the revision of the *Book of Texts* for the year, and then conversed about what God had done for him and for the community for thirty years.

"Who would have thought at the beginning," said he to David Nitschmann and a few other old men, "that the Savior would have done what He has done for us and for the other Churches and for the heathen? As for the heathen I only asked for the first-fruits, and, behold, a harvest!"

His friends began to hope that the fever was abating and that he might yet be spared to them; but, at midnight, his tongue began to swell, and he was in danger of suffocation. Early in the morning, about a hundred of the Brethren and sisters gathered at his bedside and in the adjacent rooms.

The Count raised his eyes towards them and looked at them, but could not speak. They responded with tears to this silent benediction. The farewell glance was very solemn, and affected every heart. The end was drawing near. At nine o'clock, John Watteville broke the silence with the words: "Lord, lettest Thou Thy servant, now depart in peace!" Then, placing his hands upon the head of Zinzendorf, he pronounced the priestly benediction: "The Lord bless thee and keep thee! The Lord mercifully with His favor look upon thee! The Lord lift up His countenance upon thee, and give thee peace!" At this word "peace," the spirit passed away. It was the 9th of May, 1760. The text for the day was: "He shall doubtless come again rejoicing, bringing his sheaves with him."

A week later, his body was beautifully buried in the little graveyard on the Houtberg, amid the tears of thousands, old and young, whom he had blessed, and amid prevailing hymns of thankfulness and praise. The Brethren placed above his tomb a stone on which we read:

> Here lies the body of a man of God whose memory will never be effaced, Nicholas Louis, Count and Signior of Zinzendorf and Pottendorf, the most worthy Ordinarius of the Unity of the Brethren, restored in the 18th century by the grace of God and by his faithful and unwearied services. He was born at Dresden on the 26th of May, 1700, and entered into the joy of his Lord on the 9th of May, 1760. "I have ordained you, that ye should go and bring forth fruit, and that your fruit should remain" (John 15:16).

On the 11th of July a funeral service in honor of the Count was held at Berthelsdorf. The text of the funeral sermon was: "By the grace of God, I am what I am: and His grace was not in vain; but I labored more abundantly than they all: yet not I, but the grace of God which was with me" (1 Cor. 15:10).

Zinzendorf had, by his first marriage, twelve children, most of whom died in infancy. Three daughters survived him—Benigna, the wife of John de Watteville; Mary Agnes; and Elizabeth, who married the Baron Frederick de Watteville, son of Nicholas. The only surviving descendants of the Count sprang from Benigna. Many of them are members of the Moravian Churches in America. His second wife, Anna Nitschmann, only survived him a few days. She was buried by his side on the Houtberg.

Chapter 27

Character of the Count

Although the character of Zinzendorf shines forth from all his life and work, it may be of interest if we present two special full-length portraits of him drawn, with much discrimination and fidelity, by two biographers who knew him long and well. The first is by Spangenberg:

> The Count had a lively and a fruitful intellect. Thoughts sprang up in his mind with equal abundance and rapidity. In meditation and in intellectual toil he was indefatigable. His mind produced a multitude of original ideas which he often clothed in strange and startling forms. He was also singularly inventive when some useful enterprise was needed, and new means of executing them were required, and he would then express himself with great vivacity. His memory was prompt and comprehensive, but it could not always be depended on for details.
>
> He was naturally so alert and active that it was difficult for him to be idle. He did not know how to work slowly, and, when he had once taken a thing in hand, he could not rest till it was finished: he put into it all his powers. He did not like to be interrupted, but when this was absolutely necessary, he could quickly and entirely turn to the new affair; but it was difficult for him to take up again the business he had left.
>
> So far as I can judge, his temperament was very similar, in many points, to that of Luther. His feelings were strong and vehement, and easily carried him too far. Charity sometimes made him too indulgent, and zeal too severe. Sorrow affected him too deeply, and joy, though it did not put him altogether off the balance, took entire possession of his soul. If he became uneasy about something or some one, he represented things to himself in the worst light with all their consequences, and it was not easy to get him to listen to reason. When he maintained a point about which he had a profound

conviction, he ill brooked contradiction; but, on further reflection, he would often profit by the objections that had been raised.

He could not understand how men could keep to the opinions they had once formed, at all costs, and make no progress in knowledge. He thought it impossible that a man who sought for truth should not discover that of which he was ignorant and that in which he had been wrong. The love of truth demands, he thought, that one should leave that which he has when he has found something better. When it was objected that this way of thinking betrayed an inconstant character, he replied that one ought to prefer truth to a reputation for constancy, and that one ought to learn how always to remain a scholar, and to be always seeking something better. This is why he made so many alterations in his writings. He never ceased correcting them. When any one else pointed out a phrase that did not run quite smoothly and suggested an improvement, he received it with the utmost pleasure, and when he himself hit upon a happy turn of expression, or a word that more completely expressed his meaning, he rejoiced over it like a little child.

Whenever he met with men in whom there was the faintest love to the Savior, or the first beginnings of the Holy Spirit's work, he was at once at home with them, no matter what religion they were of, or what were their opinions with respect to other things. He had quite an exceptional talent for conversing with men who did not think like him. He always managed to express his opinions clearly and frankly, and yet without offence. Still, before he had had much experience, he would concede sometimes too much, sometimes too little, and he often showed more consideration for men than they merited.

As the incarnation, sufferings, and death of Jesus were the subjects which filled his heart, so they formed the staple of his conversations and discourses. In the ordinary intercourse of life, he was as simple and transparent as a child. One saw in him what a beautiful thing it is to be freed by the blood of Jesus from the fears inspired by a conscience ill at ease. All his actions, all his words bore witness to his tender love for Christ his Savior, for all the members of His Body, for all the souls that He has ransomed at a price so vast. He was friendly, cordial, unsuspicious, frank, at peace with all men. It was for him a real pleasure to be of any service to others. He made no difference, in doing good, between friends and enemies, unless it was to show the preference to his foes.

He had acquired, as much by reading history and Scripture as by experience, a profound knowledge of the human heart. Frequently he fell into grave disquietude respecting some of his dearest friends, and, as he could not help speaking, it was often very painful both for him and them. It was not enough that they avoided positive evil; he was anxious that they should avoid the appearance of evil, whatever might become the occasion of sin. His solicitude extended to every member of the community, even to the little children, and had reference to every thing, even to what might have appeared most insignificant. He occupied himself by preference, with those who were miserable, simpleminded, and ungifted, and who, for this reason, were of no account to other men. When he found in such persons a true love to the Savior, he had for them a peculiar affection and esteem.

The other portrait is by Schrautenbach:

Zinzendorf was not free from faults, but all who knew him witness to his keen perception of the truth and to his fidelity in following and serving it. He was always equal to himself, so far as his principles were concerned, and the object he had in view. This quality, *unum hominem agere* ("to thine own self be true"), so uncommon among men, was throughout his life his distinguishing characteristic.

With his activity, his genius, his varied faculties, one ought not to be surprised to find in him some oddities, some apparent contradictions. Those who knew him intimately knew him to be fundamentally loyal. This loyalty breathed in all his words, and manifested itself both in ordinary life and in the decisive moments of his history. And yet one can hardly read Tacitus without being reminded of him. One noticed in him something of the wary politician, something like equivocation, and, at times, dissimulation; a certain over-anxiety to maintain his authority, even when no one disputed it. These were traits arising, partly from his character and education, and partly from the courtly atmosphere that he had breathed. The Brethren were quite familiar with these features in the Count, but they did not detract from the profound consideration in which he was held and the unbounded confidence that he inspired. They were more a matter of form and manner than of character.

What specially distinguished him was his zeal for the public good, his benevolence, his energy, his constancy, the nobility of his soul, his disinterestedness, his persistent devotion of his life to elevated ends Never was a man more beloved by his friends; never, however, was a character more often analyzed and pulled to pieces; but his merits easily survived each new examination. The angles and projections in his character only add to our interest in studying it. His creative genius, his faculty of observation, his comprehensive glance, enabled him to see things in an unaccustomed and an unexpected light. In his discourses he seldom seized on what others would have thought the salient points; they were always improvised, and often striking and original. It was the same in his affairs; one never knew by what end he would lay hold of them, but one was always sure that it was the end by which he meant to carry them. That in all these matters he should always have kept within the bounds of moderation is more than we could expect from a nature so rich, placed in a situation so exceptional. With a sphere of action so wide, a sphere on which, literally, the sun never set, it would have been impossible for him to transact his affairs as minutely and methodically as a man with only one thing to do....

Action—that essential quality for the orator—the eloquence of gesture and of voice, were never wanting, and were quite natural to him. He had a manly voice, full, harmonious, expressive. The difficult art of giving to each word its proper intonation, of suiting the expression and the attitude to the word, and all this unconsciously and without exciting observation, he naturally possessed. One felt that there was soul, life, harmony, in all he did. In his personal appearance there was grandeur, force, nobility, distinction.... In his dress he was simple in the extreme, sometimes careless. He was always badly lodged, indifferent about furniture, never seeking comfort, and utterly devoid of whims, and fads, and fantasies. He had few needs, and in all that pertained to his person, his food, his clothes, he was both plain and simple and incorrigible. Nevertheless, there was a certain elegance in his bearing, and something reserved in his manners. He had plenty of smiles for those with whom he was familiar, but he knew how to be stern, and distant, and intimidating. Many a one has gone to speak to him, and has returned without being able to remember what they had gone to say. Nevertheless, the Count was ordinarily cheerful, chatty, affable. He loved an innocent raillery, even when he himself was the object of it; but no one was familiar, or took liberties with him. They loved him, honored him, but, when in his presence, they always felt that they were with a man of rank.... "I have a spirit as much inclined to extravagance as any man," he says in one of his writings. The avowal does him honor. We could hardly have expected it from a man who has been accused of seeking to make men worship him.

Since we have spoken of his manner of conducting himself towards his brethren and fellow-workers, we ought not to omit his mania for grumbling, sometimes a disagreeable mania. He would grumble, for example, if a form in the church was not placed as he desired.... But it is to be remarked that he never used cutting words or undignified expressions. These little explosions were probably, with him, a physical necessity; but he often checked himself with some such remark as, "Do not make me more ridiculous than I am."

As for his knowledge, he had acquired it almost all himself. Latterly, he read hardly anything but the Bible. For the last twenty years of his life I do not believe he read a single religious book. He wrote much, and meditated much. It has been said, with some reason, that his works abound in loose and careless expressions. This is true of the discourses that were printed from the notes of his hearers. All his works have not the same value, and some of them had better not have been published. But in many of them there is a mine of truth, of theology, of rules of conduct, of knowledge of God and man. They are not finished works (his mind was too lively to continue long at work on the same task); they are rather essays. But you will find few orators whose discourses, though so little prepared, are so rich in thought and sentiment, or who, in constantly treating of only one thing, present it under so many different aspects.

One of the most beautiful traits in his character was his immovable faith in "that which is written." He was perfectly familiar with all the doubts that may be raised with respect to the Bible. The way in which such doubts are usually answered did not altogether satisfy him. In his youth he had read Bayle, and many authors of a kind. He did not deny there *might* be historical or chronological errors in our copies of the Scriptures. He did not believe in what is known as "verbal inspiration." But his whole system rests upon the Bible as the Book of God, the revelation which contains the Divine counsel for the salvation of men.

www.ingramcontent.com/pod-product-compliance
Lightning Source LLC
La Vergne TN
LVHW050936080826
845145LV00004B/1286

* 9 7 8 1 9 3 2 7 7 4 3 8 2 *